SKETCHES OF GRANGE
AND
THE NEIGHBOURHOOD
(1850)

with a new introduction

by

ROBIN WEBSTER

Landy Publishing
2001

Originally published in 1850, this is a photographical facsimile reprint with some contemporary illustrations added, along with a new introduction by Robin Webster.

The terms of the Copyright, Designs and Patents Act 1988 and the Duration of Copyright & Rights in Performances Regulations 1995 are to be applied.

ISBN 1 872895 56 5

British Library in Cataloguing Publication Data.
A catalogue record of this book is available from the British Library.

Layout by Mike Clarke: 01254 395848
Printed by Nayler the Printer Ltd., Accrington: 01254 234247

Landy Publishing have also published:

Cockersand Abbey by Brian Marshall
A History of Pilling by F. J. Sobee
Rishton Remembered by Kathleen Broderick
A Blackburn Childhood in Wartime by Marjorie Clayton
An Accrington Mixture edited by Bob Dobson
A Blackburn Miscellany edited by Bob Dobson
Blackburn in Times Gone By compiled by Jim Halsall
Bolland Forest and the Hodder Valley by Greenwood and Bolton
Blackburn's Shops at the Turn of the Century by Matthew Cole
Sand Grown (Lytham St. Annes) by Kathleen Eyre

A full list is available from:

Landy Publishing
'Acorns' 3 Staining Rise, Staining, Blackpool, FY3 0BU
Tel/Fax: 01253 895678

INTRODUCTION

Sketches of Grange is a series of letters, which were published in the *Kendal Mercury*, by John Hudson in the late 1840s. They were produced from an earlier volume of 1848 published by George Lee of Finkle Street, Kendal, entitled *A Guide to Grange*. There is, however, no reference to George Lee in the *History of Westmorland with Furness and Cartmel* under the sections 'newspapers and printers' and 'letter press' in 1849. He is not mentioned in similar sections in Pigot's *Directory of Westmorland* in 1829. John Hudson is noted as being in partnership with Cornelius Nicholson at that time. Later, these 'letters', by various authors, were re-published as this book to raise money for the building of St. Paul's Church in Grange. Unbeknown to its authors, the sketches were to provide us with a remarkable insight into Grange and district in the mid-nineteenth century.

John Hudson was born in Ambleside in 1799. He traded as **Hudson and Nicholson** as printer, bookseller, bookbinder, stationer and newsagent on Highgate in Kendal. He was an apprentice with Richard Lough, who was also a printer in Kendal, and Cornelius Nicholson. The latter became his brother-in-law. From 1845 to 1846 he was agent for the *Liverpool Mercury*. In 1861 the firm was taken over by Hudson's apprentice and traded under his name, Titus Wilson. Hudson then concentrated on the manufacture of paper. He had at one time an interest in the Cowanhead Paper Mill and the Burneside Paper Mill.

The first reference to Grange can be found in 1490 when Henry VII was on the throne. In 1536, (Henry VIII) *Grange with Kentisbank* is detailed in the Cartmel Priory Registers. The John Spede map of Lancashire, 1577 (Elizabeth I), shows the *Carters Lonnye Crossing* indicating a right of way across Morecambe Bay. By 1684, Charles II was King and parts of the village of Cartmel and Grange were shown on Widow Houseman's map. The warehouse, with a Coast Officer employed, was built in 1729. Around 1730 (George II), the Bay Horse (now Commodore Hotel) was built and this was followed nearly sixty years later when the Crown Hotel was built on the site of Crown Hill Flats. 1832 (William IV) saw the erection of a house on Holme

Island, and during Queen Victoria's reign, in 1841, Eggerslack Cottage was built.

The Census for 1851 shows there were forty houses at Grange. These stretched from Spring Bank Farm down Windy Harbour, which was sited approximately around what is now the Grange Hotel and the railway station. The only properties left today are: Spring Bank Farm, Woodheads, Hardcragg Hall, Grange House, Bay Villa, Myrtle Cottage, The Commodore Hotel, Cragg Cottage and some of the fishing cottages around Eggerslack Terrace. Kent's Bank Road, Main Street, Fernhill Road did not exist but it is likely that there was a track which lead down from Eggerslack following the road which is now Main Street, leading up Grange Fell Road and over to Cartmel, past Hardcragg Hall and Woodheads Farm. The road from Lindale came past Lindale Church and threaded its way through Eggerslack, possibly entering Grange at Windermere Road. Some evidence suggests the name of the track could have been 'Pepper Lane'. There will also have been a track leading to Cart Lane and the Guide's House. In 1851 there were 188 people living in Grange: 52 men, 66 women and 70 children. The occupations included brewer, farmer, agricultural worker, tailor, stone mason, coachman, wood hoop maker, laundress, innkeeper, retired master mariner, seed and spice merchant, butcher and paper cordwainer. 'Landed proprietor' appeared several times. Surprisingly, there were no fishermen recorded.

It has been established that the site of the granary from which Grange derived its name was situated at John Brough's Farm, later to become the first Police Station. The granary belonged to Cartmel Priory and was used for storing cargo brought by boat. In 1851, the farm was fifty-five acres and Brough employed one farm labourer. He lived with his wife Isabella and his daughter of three, Mary. His wife and daughter were born at Crosthwaite and John came from Leak (*sic* – Leck?) in Yorkshire.

Inhabitants of Grange came from as far afield as Sidmouth in Devon, Manchester, Liverpool and Scarborough. Howere if it had not been for Sarah Ann Clarke of Liverpool, the book you are about to read would never have been printed. Miss Clarke was staying with the Wright family at Bay Villa. She had taught one of their three children and was visiting Grange on holiday. She was not happy that a number of the poor mothers of the village could not spare the time to go to church at either Lindale or Cartmel, so she set to, raising funds to build a church at Grange. *Sketches of Grange* formed a part of the fund raising, supported by the Earl of Burlington and a Mr. Wakefield. Miss Susanna Newby gave part of her garden and the church was built on what was known as 'The Ha' which roughly translates as 'Heartland'.

'Quaecunque Amabilia Cognitate' is part of the Grange Coat of Arms. Its literal translation is 'Think on that which is Beautiful'. The book epitomises this motto and as you read each page, enjoy the journey around Grange and district during the middle of the nineteenth century.

Robin Webster
Grange over Sands
June 2001

SKETCHES

OF

GRANGE

AND

The Neighbourhood.

KENDAL:

PRINTED BY JOHN HUDSON.

—

1850.

J. Webster delt.

Hutchins Lithog.r Liverpool.

Cramond

Introduction.

HE following Sketches of Grange originally appeared in the literary corner of the *Kendal Mercury*, and may require some introduction on presenting themselves in the more independent character which they have been politely requested to assume by some of those who honoured them with a degree of approval to which they scarcely aspired.

The favourable notice they have received must be chiefly attributed to the attractiveness of the scenery which they endeavour to describe, and those readers who may be stimulated to explore more carefully the secluded glens and vallies of the neighbourhood, may feel assured that a rich reward awaits them, and that these slight outlines are susceptible of an infinite variety of detail.

But the most persuasive plea for a second appearance remains to be mentioned, and upon it must rest the chief apology for giving to papers of a fugitive character a form more permanent than was originally contemplated. Efforts are now making to supply the inhabitants of Grange and its vicinity with a Church. To aid this most desirable object the promoters have invited the publication of these selections, and although doubts may shadow the author's mind as to the profitable result of so small a volume, the proposal to reprint it for such an object has been most cheerfully complied with.

SKETCHES AT GRANGE.

CHAPTER I.

ARRIVAL.—APPEARANCE.—HOLME ISLAND.

GRANGE-OVER-SANDS FROM HOLME ISLAND.

CHAPTER I.

In these days, when the English reader may learn all that the most accomplished tourist can distil from the banks of the Rhine, the Lakes of Switzerland, and the waters of the Bosphorus, by studying at home a few of the numerous works which, under the form of " Tours," " Letters," or " Hand-books," issue from the press in Albermarle-street, who shall blame an humble attempt to to point out to the less aspiring traveller, some of the attractions to be found in the neighbourhood of one of the loveliest spots in the Queen's dominions ?

The beautiful Village of Grange, whose charms this little volume is intended to describe, is situated on Morecambe Bay, on the west side of the Estuary formed by the waters of the river Kent. It has acquired celebrity not only from the beauty of its scenery, but from the mildness of its climate, which rivals that of the southern coast of England. Its sheltered site knows little of the inclement blasts which neighbouring districts experience in the winter; for it lies, or rather hangs, on the southern declivity of a mountain limestone range, which shelters it from the north and west. In spring its temperature is higher on the average than any other place in the north of England, and in summer the heat is tempered by the breezes which blow land-ward or sea-ward with the flow and ebb of the tide.

A glance at the Map will convince any one, that although Grange is withdrawn from the great thoroughfares of the country, it is very easy of access, and the approaches are in themselves sufficiently attractive to reward the attempt. The ordinary route either from the north or south commences with Levens Bridge, about five miles to the south of Kendal, and opens with an extensive view of that magnificent escarpment of rock, Whitbarrow Scar, which lifts its hoary head as if a rival of Underbarrow Scar, the two forming a giant-like gateway, through which the cloud-capt mountains at the head of Windermere are seen A rich foreground of cultivated moss completes a picture of no common interest.

The tract of country at the head of Morecambe Bay, known as " the Mosses," must not be passed over without notice. To a southern eye they are a new and interesting feature in the landscape. Here the peasantry procure their chief supply of fuel, and, at the time of peat harvest, hundreds of acres of black bog are thickly overspread with a hard-working sun-browned population, cutting, drying, or storing the peat. These valuable beds of fuel are many feet in depth, and are very systematically cut perpendicularly in thin slices and then divided into pieces about the size of a brick. To hasten the process of drying, they are carefully piled in small stacks, the " peats" being so arranged as to be fully exposed to the action of the sun and wind. In many parts of the peat-moss large trunks of trees are discovered, and prove that these extensive plains of fuel are the remains of immense forests, which either once stood where they now lie, or were washed down from the recesses of the hills, or were stranded by tidal currents, having been borne by the ocean from other lands. The subject is one which we commend to the investigation of the curious.

The road to Grange crosses these mosses, and was peculiar, a long time after its formation, for its undulating or quivering motion, which was very perceptible when any heavy vehicle passed along it. In its construction an enormous quantity of earth was swallowed up in the bog soil, before the foundation was deemed sufficiently solid, but the difficulty was at last surmounted, and an excellent highway is the result.

Passing under Whitbarrow Scar, near to Castle Head, through Lindale, and over Blawith Hill, shadowed by Eggerslack wood, all which places we hope to describe, as being well worthy the attention of the stranger, we descend a steep hill, and find ourselves in the sweet village of Grange.

By this route, at the close of a brilliant day about the middle of May, and after a long journey, we reached our quarters. They were of no lordly dimensions, or metropolitan grandeur, such as are to be found at what are called "watering places," in the south of England. Like the other nooks in this quiet spot, our temporary domicile proved a small—very small—cottage, but possessed of every needful comfort. Lovely roses in full perfection clustered round the windows, and mingled with the ivy and other climbers which decorated the rustic porch. And well did the plain and simple accommodations of the interior jus-

tify this attractive invitation to enter : but more on this
subject presently.

Those only who know the incessant restlessness (a
north man would call it bustle) which extends beyond the
suburbs of London to what a *citizen* calls "the country,"
can have an idea of the delight which filled our mind as
we contemplated the calm beauty that met our awakening
gaze on the morrow of our arrival. A landscape more
suggestive of repose cannot be conceived. All was soft,
peaceful, and serene, and yet, from the variety of objects
in view, and the constant change produced by the ebb and
flow of the tide, with the ever-varying effect of cloud and
sunlight, it never can become insipid to any real lover of
nature.

There is life breathing over those sands, now dry, now
hid from sight by the stormy or tranquil waters. There
is a voice in those swelling woods, when their deep stillness seems the very emblem of silence, or when their
rustling leaves whisper that the cool airs are astir, or their
murmurs tell us that the sea breeze, the advent messenger
of the tide or of the tempest, is amongst them. Those
rocks also speak to the soul, for the expression of their
outline is eloquent of beauty, as ridge beyond ridge
stretches out into the Bay, each point becoming mellowed
into softness by the sunset glow, and each little promontory tinged with its own peculiar hue, more and
more delicate as it recedes in the distance, till the form of
the coast line is lost in a bright silvery haze ; at other
times they grow black and grim or gloomy, as the clouds
of heaven are portentous of the angry storm or tempest.
In general there is little in the view to impress the mind
with awe or wonder, but surely such scenes are calcu-

lated to elevate the thoughts to Him who permits us the enjoyment of so fair a world.

From the Sands—which form a delightful promenade, and upon which the visitor may safely walk with the exercise of ordinary watchfulness against the insidious approach of the advancing tide—the view of Grange is peculiarly attractive. No stately terraces of "commodious" lodging-houses disturb the rural character of the scene. A few lovely residences of a superior order, embosomed in plantations, attract the attention, but good taste has presided over their erection, and they harmonize well with surrounding objects.

The Hotel, which has lately been enlarged, occupies a commanding situation, and we believe that it well deserves the patronage it receives from the visitors to Grange. The views from its windows are delightful. But the scattered white cottages, which properly compose the village, are the most picturesque objects. They appear to nestle among the foliage of the rich woods which clothe the side of the steep hill on which the hamlet rises, whilst in some places, the dwellings are so close to the shore, that at high-tide you may look down from the windows into the waters below. The whole coast of this estuary presents an amphitheatre of beauty. On the east side pretty villages adorn the little recesses, formed by the projecting points of the high land, and as these are viewed from different positions there is an ever-changing variety in the detail. On the western side the view is bounded by the bold promontory of Humphrey Head, whose deep broad shadow, cast upon the waters at Wyke bay, is a fitting foreground to our picture.

Perhaps the object which first arrests the stranger's

eye, as it wanders over this charming scene, is HOLME ISLAND. Situated near the head of the Bay, it appears from Grange to form the centre of the amphitheatre. Its area is small, comprising not more than eleven acres, but in that limited space every thing has been done to make the resources of art minister to the advantageous display of the beauties of nature. At the time of our visit the owner of this lovely spot was leaving the country, and hearing that a sale of the furniture, &c. was to take place, and that consequently it was open to the public, we resolved to visit it. We had a pleasant drive of about a mile over the Sands, and found the crossing of the channel safe,—a state of things not always to be calculated upon, as, without care, carriages are sometimes caught in the quicksands.

Immediately upon passing the entrance gate you find yourself in a highly-cultivated garden. Rhododendrons and laurels skirt the carriage drive, and screen large beds of azaleas and other choice American plants, tastefully selected and arranged. They appear to flourish in great perfection, and were all in full bloom and beauty.

The house is a low range of building, in a fanciful style of architecture, the reception-rooms and principal bed-rooms being all on one story. The entrance is formed by a handsome flight of steps leading into a small conservatory, in which were a few articles of taste, and a very fine orange tree in full flower, whose rich and penetrating odour shed a perfume throughout the apartments. A small octagon room, fitted up in a simple manner, introduced us to the drawing-room, where the many costly and beautiful accessories to a really elegant apartment were displayed for the gratification of the curious, in all the admired

HOLME ISLAND

C. Hunchms Lithographer, Liverpool

GRANGE FROM BLAWITH POINT

confusion usual on such occasions. The most incongruous articles were heaped together for the convenience of purchasers anxious for a close inspection—window-curtains, footstools, and druggets, &c. &c., piled upon chairs and sofas, which were evidently never intended to bear such common-place burdens ; things that ought to be upon the floor placed upon the costly inlaid tables, and things intended to grace the table placed upon the floor. There were a few beautiful carvings in ivory, some casts, foreign glass, and a small collection of articles of vertû, but nothing very striking. The dining-room we thought very handsome, though some might consider its fair proportions were marred by its great length. But the views from the windows are beautiful, and the *coup d'œil*—when the folding-doors are thrown open, and the sliding panels into a large conservatory at one end are drawn back, allowing the eye to pass along the whole suite of apartments—is quite magical. *Fairy*-like it certainly is, for all is so bright and gay and glittering, and on so small a scale, that the resemblance naturally suggests itself.

Turning from the scene in the interior, where every variety of domestic utensil was shortly to be submitted to the business-like competition of ladies and gentlemen, we gladly made our escape to the gardens, which are laid out with great taste, and lavishly planted with choice trees and shrubs. Winding walks on the face of the rocky cliffs conduct to summer-houses of various forms and sizes, some intended for the social party, and others for the more select. Some of them overhang the tide, and are charmingly placed so as to command the best views of the surrounding scenery. We were pleased to observe that the wild plants of the district have been located in favourable

situations among these rocky paths—all carefully labelled
and named—an undertaking which does great credit to
the taste of whoever designed it.   On the southern point
of the island, a Grecian Temple has been erected, at a
prodigious cost, we understand.   We had thought it ornamental when viewed from the opposite shore, but it
struck us, when near, as an error in taste, and, though
beautiful as a building, very much out of place.   It is
encompassed by a miniature ditch, which is crossed by a
formidable-looking bridge ; but in the place of water you
gaze upon a flower-bed, filled with blossoms of every hue,
and which circles this "model temple of Vesta" like a
radiant garland.   The plantations are well arranged, and
several rare pines seem to flourish.   For a temporary residence during the summer Holme Island is doubtless a
very pleasant place, but, like most earthly paradises, it has
its drawbacks.   This "gem of the sea" possesses *no
springs of water*, and, to those who value a good pump
more than good wine, this is a serious objection.   How
the deficiency has been supplied we know not ; probably
by contributions from the clouds, or by substituting those
from the wine cellar.   After a delightful ramble in the
gardens, we again crossed the Sands, now glowing beneath the setting sun, and presenting a richness and
variety of colouring which it were a vain attempt to describe.   But we were reminded that its now brilliant
golden surface, like much of the glory of this world, concealed beneath it treacherous quicksands, which, with the
uncertain tide, were the inevitable contingencies upon a
residence at this lovely Island, lovely in itself, and lovely
as an object from the charming village of Grange.

CHAPTER II.

YEWBARROW AND HAMPSFELL.

GRANGE-OVER-SANDS FROM YEWBARROW.

CHAPTER II.

At the summit of the limestone range, on the side of which Grange is perched, there stands a rude pile of stones commemorating the birth of some owner of the property. A gradual acclivity on three sides renders it easy of access. On the south it has a terraced, and, in some places, an almost perpendicular escarpment—a face common on one side to nearly all the limestone in the district. Along the terraces there are beautiful ascending walks, overhung with rocks which abound with fossil remains of a primeval world. They are inclosed within the grounds of Yew-barrow Cottage, belonging to Miss Hall. This residence commands an extensive prospect, and is snugly sheltered from every blast. It only wants the vines and the more delicate creepers, and the villa style of Italy, to remind the gazer, at a full tide, of one of those spots which over-hang the Bay of Naples.

The terrace approach to the summit being private, the visitor must pass through a gate adjoining a charming little well of pellucid water, whose coolness might indicate distillation from an internal glacier. Near the gate there is a rustic thatched cottage, which, like the nest of the stonefinch, appears as if *growing* upon the rock. Here the visitor may ask for directions, which will guide him amongst masses of limestone, strewed hither and thither, and chiselled by the rain and weather in a manner unequalled by any mason's tool. They are used in the front of Yewbarrow Lodge, the beautiful residence of Wm. Hargreaves, Esq. and in the marine villa belonging to George Webster, Esq. Winding amongst these rocks, and through ferns of luxuriant growth, and over a downy sod, soft as velvet, the path reaches the summit of Yewbarrow.

The name of the hill indicates its character. Barrow is a pile or mass of loose stones, and comprehends the cairn of the ancient British King, and the magnificent masses of rock which bear this name, at the waterfall near Keswick, at Whitbarrow, Underbarrow, Katbarrow, &c.

The student of history loves these old names. They tell him of days gone by, when a scout stood upon each lofty summit, if danger was nigh. Besides him was reared the pile of faggots, and on the ground was the smouldering turf, ready to kindle the beacon-light into a flame, on the approach of the foe. On the ground lay his bow made of the well-known yew tree, which flourishes abundantly at Grange, and which gives the adjunct to the name of this summit.

From Yewbarrow the eye-range is elaborate, beginning at the moorlands of Shap Fell—including Ingleborough, far away in Yorkshire,—over Arnside and Farleton Knots, all, like itself, ancient beacon heights, to the distant country of the Fylde below Lancashire, and which stretches out for miles and miles on the horizon, only just lifted up above the surface of the sea.

A VIEW FROM THE ROCKS NEAR GRANGE.

C. Hullmandel Lithographer. Little Queen.

Yewbarrow is a pleasant evening's walk, for the sunlight upon the opposite shore paints the landscape with a brilliancy which almost rivals the vividness of eastern colouring, and which is probably derived from the reflection of some of the rays of light from the wide expanse of sand which intervenes between the eye and the distant objects. An acquaintance with the sands elicits a great many instances of optical singularity, to some of which we shall have to refer.

But the visitor to Grange must not be satisfied with Yewbarrow. There is a higher ascent, and as he stands on the lower, though it is an elevated point, his thoughts and aims climb upward, and he resolves to achieve the loftier summit. A day is set down for the ascent of Hampsfell, and the weather is watched for its accomplishment. The sagacious host of the Hotel expresses serious doubts, by significant intimations of the head, when you consult him on the morning of the appointed day. And if you ask old James, he answers, as he gives a half upward and half side-long glance at the sky—" Whya, sur, neaboddy kens mich aboot it, but mebbie it'ill hod oot ower t'day." It does hold out, though dense masses of clouds float in the heavens, while, between them, the large spaces of deep Tyrian blue look like the portals to a world pure but sublime. The weather has long been dry. The sun is burning hot whenever he throws off his beams out of those cerulean portals, silvering with brilliancy the edges of the surrounding clouds.

A breeze from the tide strays up among the woods, rustling their leaves, but looses its way before reaching the lady-fern on the fell, which bends only to the weight of the beetle, or the light leap of the grasshopper.

Lunch, but don't dine, when you climb a hill!—At four
o'clock send up the feeble ones of the party by a steep
carriage-road which skirts the south side of Eggerslack
wood, and on the open fell you can drive very nearly to the
summit. Let the ramblers proceed on the Lindale road,
but refuse the tempting coppice which invites them on
their left hand, almost buried in which stands Eggerslack Cottage, built by John Wakefield, Esq., of Sedgwick,
a picturesque spot, and which—quite apropos to the situation—has its floors formed of larchwood, set perpendicularly in honey-comb fashion.

The entrance to Eggerslack wood is at the farm-house
called the Slack. Here is another ancient name, which
signifies a hollow between hills. It is the root of the
compound name of the wood, which was probably at first
"higher," or "heigher," (in the provincial pronunciation)
"slack,"—a suitable descriptive name of the "Higher hollow." Some derive it from Agger, but no fortification
seems to have been discovered near it. Before entering
it, it may be well to describe this romantic glen.

The coppice woods and larch plantations of Westmorland and Furness are sources of considerable wealth, and
are truly ornamental. By them a large acreage of land is
made productive, and often remunerative, which would
otherwise have been of little profit, except for grazing a
few sheep. The rugged rocks, which seem only fit to
starve, not to feed, the stock of the fell farmer, become
clothed with verdure, and the feathery larch and the rich
green spruce fir gain a hold amongst rocks, stones, and
moss, fold their roots around the large blocks like a
cable round a mooring post, and send their suckers deep
into the crevices, as if they would anchor themselves

against the wildest of winters' storms. Amongst them are planted hardwood trees, the birch, the oak, the ash, a few alder and a few beech, which, sheltered by the more rapid growing, but less hard-grained wood, gradually get hold of a home among the hills.

Besides the larch plantations, there are the oak and the hazel coppice, which, every fourteen years, fall before the woodman's axe, giving employment to a numerous set of people, who strip the former of its bark, and then burn the stems into charcoal for the gunpowder works, which are located in the romantic gorges of the neighbouring rivers. The hazel is felled for bobbin-wood, and of the nut-bearing boughs of the autumn, some are, next year, scattered among the bobbin-mills of Westmorland, to be sent, when filled with cotton thread, for the use of the lady's work-box, to every quarter of the globe—others are split up for hoops, and shipped to Liverpool, for the coopers, who make casks for that great emporium of the world ; others, under the designation of "basket rods," are sent to the busy population of Lancashire, where they are formed into the corves, or baskets, which are used for bringing up the coal and the workmen from the mines, or, when on wheels, transmitting the coal from the workings along a railroad in those underground regions, to the foot of the shafts, whence it is hoisted by the steam-engine to daylight. Eggerslack was planted with larch, as well as with coppice, by a member of a family who clothed many of the once barren hills of this district with the rich mantles which they now wear, and whose descendants are reaping the profit of their ancestor's judgment and foresight, while the lover of nature, and the naturalist also, rejoice in this profitable good taste.

It has been said that land, which cost fifteen pounds per acre for the freehold, by the yearly thinning of the plantations, and the ultimate sale on the fall of the wood, yielded four per cent. per annum, besides one hundred pounds per acre, as a return for the original investment, the land being, at the end of about sixty years, far better in quality than when first planted. Probably Eggerslack has been very productive, as it appears to be peculiarly favourable for the growth of wood.

Penetrating the farm-yard at the Slack, a steep rugged pathway meets you. Climbing this, a terrace lane is reached, which commands a lovely view to the sea, through a vista of hanging plantations. At the end of the lane a rock rises abruptly, from the foot of which a quiet glistening spring flows out, and seems to be a favorite spot of refreshment for the denizens of that wooded wilderness. Passing this, and through a gate, a new scene opens. A glen winds at the foot of rugged cliffs, almost grown up with the richest foliage, among which the hawk and the wood-pigeon build as in a native domain. The rich rank grass almost conceals the path, and soon every other prospect is closed, but that of verdure towering on every hand. It is a miniature American forest, with the prairie and the tangled jungle all on a small scale. There the multitudinous insect tribe, for which Grange is remarkable, and which are so interesting to the naturalist, abound. There the wood-cutter finds the squirrel, the rabbit and the fox. The harmless specimens of the serpent tribe find a home there. It is a place for the student or the solitary; and the group of ramblers can bask on a summer afternoon in the perfect stillness of that secluded scene.

Leaving this behind, the path opens on to the moorland,

where the soft short grass yields to the tread. The juniper bushes and the ferns grow here; and the grasshoppers and cuckoo are heard mingling their tones with the humming bee, which rejoices as it ransacks the bell of the flowering heath. Over the common the pathway is lost, but the summit is the compass of the path-finders, and on, and on they go, till they reach the highest crag, when the prospect opens out on all sides. Westward the lake mountains lose themselves in the clouds, which are settling down with the advance of day. Coniston Old Man is clear. The Langdale Pikes are below the level of the clouds; and Great End, Scawfell, and Bowfell, are become the pillars of the Heavens. What a gap Dunmail Raise shows in that mighty wall of mountains, which is only broken by the valleys which convey the water to the sea, and extends from the hills of the West Riding of Yorkshire to Black Comb, on the shores of the Irish Channel! A corner of Skiddaw rises above the deep curve of the Raise Gap, and we almost expect to see Derwentwater gleaming in the distance through the opening. Turning eastward over the valley of the Kent, the wide extent of Morecambe Bay, including the Milnthorpe and the Ulverstone estuaries from Piel to Fleetwood, are seen. And beautiful indeed is the view to the south, as the approach of even imparts its changing hues to the prospect. The vale of Cartmel lies at the feet of the beholder, the picture of repose. The town itself, clustering round its venerable church, seems at peace. It may be that the murmur of its earthly voices climbs not so high; but the musical bells of the antique Priory Church pour forth a vesper peal which floats by on melodious wings as it ascends upward and heavenward. Beyond Cartmel, in undulating ranges, the deep shaded foliage of the trees of Holker and Conishead Priory skirt and embosom the shores of the Ulverston bay. Behind these the hills of Low Furness shelter the town of Ulverston, whose blue smoke indicates its position. They also give relief to the white spire of Bardsea church, and, stretching out to the sea, terminate in the melancholy-looking Pile of Fouldry. For away beyond all, the Irish ocean gleams in the sun like a line of gold.

How fair, how surpassing fair is such a scene! and amidst the rich verdure around—the luxuriance below, and the peaceful swelling notes of those church bells—the mind glances backward over the stream of time, and involuntarily asks, " Did the landscape smile as fair when the Robber Dane built his stronghold on Piel Island, and planted his foot on this part of the British shore ?"

From this height the eye sweeps for miles on every hand over a circuit so comprehensive and varied that little is left to be wished for ; very few spots are to be met with which combine so extended and so diversified a landscape. No wonder then that the thoughtful benevolence of the Pastor of the Parish Church, like-minded with his predecessors, the Priors of the olden time, should have provided a Hospice for the shelter and refreshment of the visitor upon this Eyry of Cartmel. " Hampsfell Hospice" is inscribed on the erection. It is built of the grey limestone marble of the fell. Its architecture is not Ionic nor classical, but from its similarity to the neighbouring farm-buildings, it may be denominated the " native style." A spacious fire-place in one corner, and seats around the room, afford accommodation for the tea-kettle and its worshippers. The roof provides water, and the ferns and ling the fuel. Moreover, there is a dialogue between the host and the visitor inscribed on the walls, which reminds the guest of the converse of spirits. If there be any such haunting this moorland, even to them the door is always open ; and the rambler who complies not with the founder's request, and injures the Hospice, must take good heed to his steps as he descends the slippery sod, lest his ingratitude should receive just retribution from the fays or brownies whose rings and raths are seen on the heath grass.—The moonlight gleams serenely upon the visitor's return, the thrush and the blackbird fill the air with their rich solos, and the solemnity of evening steals over the soul, calming the spirit with its influence, and bringing out of the human heart, by its soft uniting power, some reflection of that good-will to mankind which fills the courts of Heaven, and is still manifested in the loveliness of nature's handiwork.

CHAPTER III.

CARTMEL CHURCH.

CARTMEL CHURCH

CHAPTER III.

" How soft the music of those village bells,
  Falling at intervals upon the ear
  In cadence sweet ! now dying all away,
  Now pealing loud again and louder still,
  Clear and sonorous as the gale comes on."

THE admirer of Grange is forced to confess that the charm immortalized by our truly English poet in these lines is wanting here. The stillness of the Sabbath morning is not broken by the matin peal which so soothingly reminds us that the day of rest is come, when toiling, striving man may lay aside his labour, and devote the hours to the service of Him who claims them as His own, and who, knowing our frame, has mercifully set apart a frequently recurring season, when our thoughts may be freed from our worldly occupations, and fixed without distraction upon things unseen but eternal. " What church do the Grange people attend ?" I inquired of my hostess, the first Sunday after my arrival. "Some go to Lindale and some to Cartmel, Ma'am, but it is a good two miles to either, and a very uneasy road all the way. It is a sad let down to Grange to have no church, especially for the old people who cannot walk so far, and

C

in winter many of us cannot get at all when the weather is stormy. Oh what a blessing it would be if we had a nice little chapel of our own! There was a talk of one being built, but I heard there was no ground to be got to put it on, so nothing more was said about it ; and yet one thinks that ground could have been found, if the money had been quite ready. But as you are a stranger, you should go to Cartmel ; the church there is a fine old place, and everybody ought to see it."

My hostess, who gave me this advice as she prepared the breakfast table, deserves a passing notice, as an excellent specimen of the contented well-to-do class of people in this neighbourhood. She had established herself in my good opinion, very soon after my arrival, by the frank and hearty good-will with which she applied herself to promote my comfort—apparently regarding me in the light of a visitor, towards whom she felt bound to extend the duties of hospitality for the honour of her village, rather than a lodger who could only claim "attendance" stipulated for in our bond. There was no service so small, and no trouble so great, that she would not cheerfully undertake for me, and the opportunity of enlightening my ignorance, by communicating her stores of local information to her protegé was an ample reward. I was soon initiated into the mysteries of the village politics, and the few events which occurred were duly communicated.

Let it not be inferred that she was a gossip—no more than the Court Circular deserves the name—but, like other villages, the Head Inn is the Court of Grange, and the transactions which take place there are perhaps as worthy of note, oftentimes a little more curious, and certainly as interesting, as the chronicle of the walks and rides of more important little personages. In truth, I liked to hear her talk—there was a *naive* simplicity combined with a decision and independence of character which pleased me well, and her provincial accent had a homely force and vigour about it which sounded in my southern ears like an expression of the firm and hardy character which prevails generally among the dwellers in these mountain districts. It was pleasant to see her active, well-knit figure, her open countenance and clear dark eye, which looked kindly upon every one, even to the beggar, who never knocked at her door in vain, as she went about her daily business with a cheerful happy spirit. She was truly contented with her lot in life, and utterly ignorant of those stirring events in the distant world which fill the minds of so many of us with fearful apprehensions for the future, and thus rob us of present enjoyment. Often have I listened to the joyous laughter which issued from her room when her little household had assembled after the hard labours of the day, and have thought how many a dwelling, where luxury has collected every thing to gratify the senses and please the taste, was yet destitute of the true heartfelt contentment which cheered the heart of my simple-minded and benevolent hostess.

Having concluded her eulogium upon Cartmel Church, with the information that " every body liked the Rector, and that she thought I should too," she left me to decide the matter over my breakfast. It needed not her recommendation to turn the scale in favour of Cartmel, for the sacred edifices of a past age have always a great charm for me, and are never omitted in a tour, unless from strong necessity. The morning was fine and balmy, just such a Sabbath as, when amid the hum of busy men, one thinks of the day of rest, and associates it with some well-known rural village. The cuckoo's soft clear note sounded in the copses to the left-hand road we were slowly ascending, while on the right the trees became more and more thinly scattered as we skirted the confines of Hampsfell, till they disappeared altogether. The view we have described in a former chapter, and it needs now only to be peopled with the groups of church-goers, from the neighbouring villages, who assemble to worship at Cartmel. A favourite vehicle with the farmers here appears to be a cart with a moveable seat slung across it, the straps by which it is attached to the side answering in a degree the purpose of springs. Upon this seat, which is often made quite comfortable by a support for the back, and a well-stuffed cushion of wool covered with a well-worn bit of stair carpet, the seniors of the family are accommodated, while sundry little heads behind entitle the "shandry cart" to the more dignified appellation of a family carriage. No sooner do you begin to descend into the Vale of Cartmel, than the "music" from the tower of the ancient Priory Church strikes upon the ear with a cheerful inviting sound, as if to summon all within its compass to a service of holy joy and thanksgiving. There is a solemn tone, too, in the chime, which may speak of humiliation and confession, and of fervent, earnest prayer—for of no music may it more emphatically be said that "there is in souls a sympathy with sounds," than in the emotions which the church bells awaken in the mind which pauses to drink in their melody. The neat and clean little town of Cartmel is built of the native grey limestone, and the houses cling closely to each other, and all seem to emulate contiguity to the venerable church which rises in the midst, with a protecting motherly air which is quite orthodox, almost patriarchal.

The general effect of the building is imposing. The subdued tone of its massive walls speaks of many a stormy blast, and of many a scorching sun; and the variegated colouring of the lichens have added their delicate tinting to produce that indescribable but harmonious effect which imparts a beauty that belongs to age alone, and upon which we gaze with a feeling of reverential admiration withheld from the more recent erection, though it may be faultless in its architectural proportions.

Such is the charm which stirs the heart, when we look upon the face of a beloved one, whose course is nearly run—the bloom and the freshness which marked the morning of life are gone, the bright glance no longer flashes from the joy-speaking eye; but with what deep interest do we gaze upon those softened lineaments, and trace the lines of sorrow upon that loved countenance, for they tell of a spirit within which the storms and sunshine of life have purified and refined, and which looks forward with calm and patient hope to the rest which " remaineth for the people of God."

The church is built in the form of a cross, and the transept being long in proportion, it has rather a square appearance. The tower rises in the centre, and is very remarkable in its form. Indeed it may be said to be divided into two distinct parts—the bottom being a square tower placed in the ordinary manner parallel with the walls of the church, but very low, and upon this—as if it might have been an after-thought—a continuation of the tower has been placed crosswise, producing an odd and ungraceful effect. The lofty mullioned windows, the low antique porch, independently of the size of the building, which measures 157 feet from east to west, and 110 from north to south, all mark it as an edifice of no common order. Upon entering, the noble and lofty proportions of the nave strike the attention, but, alas, whitewash disfigures the walls, and some repairs to the roof have concealed the point of the Gothic arches and given it a blunted and heavy appearance. The richly-carved screen is very beautiful, and the simple style of the architecture, especially the form of some of the arches, denotes the period of its erection to have preceded the elaborate overwrought fashion of later and more degenerate taste. The centre of the church is fitted up for public worship, and the transepts are filled with pews. Some curious extempore looking galleries are erected here and there, of various heights from the floor, and apparently in a very independent spirit, as they certainly outrage all pretensions to uniformity.

The congregation were singing the morning hymn when we entered. The space near me was chiefly occupied with open pews, where the humbler classes had ranged themselves. We suppose it is the custom in this country for the men to sit on one side, and the women apart—such, at least, was the arrangement here. Their grave and serious countenances, as they listened with fixed attention to the service, was to me another proof of the earnestness of character we have before remarked. The listlessness and abstraction of manner which is too often visible in the house of God, had no place here, and whatever might be their inward feelings, their outward demeanour was most exemplary. The plain and simple attire of the women, innocent of ribbons and finery, is worthy of all imitation, and indeed the comely well-favoured persons of a great number of them need no such ornament. The gentry must not be forgotten, as they form a rather large portion of the congregation—their pleasant residences may be seen as you descend the hill into Cartmel, studding the valley in every direction. After the service, a crowd of poor persons gathered round the clerk, who was dealing out small rolls of bread from a shelf, where they had attracted my curiosity during the service, never before having witnessed this mode of dispensing posthumous charity. The worthy clerk, who, I understand, rejoices in the honour of various avocations for the benefit of his species, and whose skill and scissors improve the heads of the parishioners in the week days, as, it is to be hoped, his services assist to improve their hearts on the Sabbath, performed his duty with a glistening eye and benevolent smile, which showed that his heart was gladdened with the task.

It appears that a church was erected and a hospital established at " Carthmell " by H. Cuthbert, of pious memory, who dedicated it to St. Mary. But, as both the church and hospital were transferred, with all their revenues, to the Priory which was founded in 1188, we must look to that period as the time when the present church was built.

There are many ancient and curious monuments in and about Cartmel Church, which illustrate the pedigrees of the families connected with the neighbourhood. One of the most ancient is the tomb-stone of William de Walton, Prior of Cartmel. He is mentioned in the Confirmation diploma of Edward II., and must have been one of the first who bore the office. Opposite to this is a magnificent tomb which must attract the attention of the curious.

Pennant thinks it belongs to Sir John Harrington, who lived about the year 1305. Sir Daniel Fleming attributes it to a Sir John de Harrington, called John of Cartmel, or his son, who lived at Wraysholme Tower. A monument in the south aisle, of a modern date, commemorates one of those affecting domestic tragedies which touch the sympathies of every heart. The story is simple, and is well told upon the marble :—A little boy, the only child of his parents, was trusted to hold the reins whilst his mother made a call. His aunt was with him in the chaise, when suddenly the horse took fright, the child was thrown out and killed upon the spot. The aunt is represented in the bas relief taking up the lifeless corpse, whilst, behind, the shadowy spirit is seen winging its way upwards. But the sound practical sermon is over, the benediction reverently spoken, the grey-headed weather-beaten labourers have left the church, the gentry have paced with becoming dignity after them, and the stamping and pattering of the numerous school children, as they rushed out last, has died away; and the sight of the ponderous old key tells us that if we would not be locked in we must linger in this hallowed pile no longer.

Appendix to Chapter iii.

APPENDIX TO CHAPTER III.

WE are gratified by learning, that since the visit to Cartmel Church alluded to in the foregoing pages, something has been done towards the renovation of that venerable edifice. The highly-respected incumbent, the Rev. Thomas Remington, animated by a laudable zeal for the restoration of sound principles of Ecclesiastical Architecture, has, by persevering energy, obtained among his friends such an amount of funds as, aided by resources at his own disposal, have enabled him to set to work the busy hand of improvement. During the last winter (1849-50) the four noble pointed arches and pillars, as well as a range on the south side of the nave, have been thoroughly cleansed from the thick coats of whitewash with which the bad taste of later times had incrusted them. They, with their bold mouldings and sculptured foliage, now stand out in all their original sharpness; whilst the removal of the decayed plaster ceiling from the centre tower, and the substitution of a boldly-designed quatrefoil-pannelled one of timber, stained dark oak colour, gives to this portion of the sacred structure its original tone, harmonizing with the richly-carved oak screen of the chancel, stalls, &c. This ceiling consists of twenty-five compartments, divided by very deep rib-mouldings and bold sculptured bosses, charged with the heraldic badges of the Tudor reigns at each angular intersection. The centre of each pannel is charged with a shield. Four are now emblazoned. Firstly, with the arms of William Mareschal Earl of Pembroke, A. D. 1188, the original founder of this Priory Church. These arms were fortunately discovered by George Webster, Esq. of Eller Howe (the gratuitous designer and superintender of the improvement), emblazoned in richly-stained glass in one of the south windows, but so coated with dust and cobwebs as to be undistinguishable until carefully cleaned.

Secondly, with the arms of the Prestons, of Holker, who were liberal renovators of the Church in their day.

Thirdly with the arms of the Archbishop of the Province; and, Fourthly, with those of the Bishop of the Diocese.

The remaining shields, now blank, will, it is to be hoped, ere long have to be charged with the armorial bearings of some of the resident landowners, who may be expected to lend their aid in carrying out further important repairs and restorations, still so much needed in the chancel and other parts of this venerable edifice.

The centre pannel contains a rich pendant, from which hangs the chandelier, surrounded by a garter, with this inscription in raised gilt letters :—

GLORIA IN EXCELSIS DEO. + ÆDIF. 1188. RENOV. 1850.

In the course of these improvements the points of two of the tower arches have been successfully relieved from the encumbrances so offensive to the correct eye.

CHAPTER IV.

THE SANDS.—KENT'S BANK.—HOLYWELL.

ANCIENT COACH ROAD OVER THE SANDS AT KENTS BANK.

CHAPTER IV.

The promontory of Humphrey Head, whale-like in form, and severing the Milnthorpe from the Ulverston Sands, is a conspicuous object to every visitor of Morecambe Bay. Its productivenes to the botanist, and its salutary springs are not unknown to fame. To it, then, let us bend our steps. At Cart Lane we take the Sands, and look in on the Carter, who, morning by morning the year round, goes to his daily duties, which are safely to guide all persons who, during low water, and between sunrise and sunset, seek to cross the channel.

This is an ancient office, and the satisfactory succession of the guides, who for many years have occupied the office, speaks well, both in name and profession, for *hereditary* carters. The Priory of Cartmel formerly maintained the Carter, towards which purpose it had synodals and Peter Pence allowed. Since the dissolution, the office is held by Patent of the Duchy of Lancaster, and the salary of £26 per annum is paid by the receiver-general.

Passing by several quiet-looking lodging-houses, we proceed nearly close to the beach, until we reach Kent's Bank. This is the point where the traveller leaves the

Cartmel shore to enter upon that great plain of sand, which, under the name of the "Lancaster Sands," has become well known to the public through the works of more than one eminent artist. Sometimes the number of people and conveyances, which cross from hence to Hest Bank, on the opposite shore, is so great as to present the appearance of a caravan traversing an Arabian desert, but consisting of oxen, sheep, horsemen, fishermen, carriers, chaises, gigs, coaches, &c., all in close succession, instead of the dromedaries and turbaned inhabitants of the East. Wheels and foot-prints furrow a highway upon the desert plain. The sun shines gaily on the merry passengers, and the jest or vivacious thought is flung about that waste of air and sand. But the procession, in a few hours, disappears—the tide rolls over the short-lived highway, and obliterates the furrows, leaving its own ripple mark instead,—the melody of the sea's voice and the cry of the curlew, sailing over the expanse of waters, replace the song and the wit of the passenger,—and solitary nature regains her sway.

At Kent's Bank there is an inn of moderate dimensions, possessing baths and other accommodation for the visitor. It has been erected by Miss Lambert, of Boar Bank, who has also built near it a very spacious and handsome house on the site of the ancient mansion of Abbot Hall. The latter once venerable building stood adjoining the shore, and under the shelter of Barrow Head. Its antique gables, high chimnies, and mullioned windows are still regretted by those who knew it in former years. True, the old oaken beams and floors and spacious staircase had suffered much from the effects of age ; the rats had been allowed free warren, and the grounds were over-run with brambles and nettles; but a ramble about its precincts, and a pilgrimage through its rooms, are among the cherished reminiscences of those who visited this locality in their youthful days. There were traditions, too, of fair and beautiful ghosts, said to haunt the place, which gave it an additional interest. Relations they were said to be of a certain Abbot who lived in retirement here, when he needed relaxation from his duties elsewhere. But these rumours received no confirmation from the actual appearance of these shadowy inmates of the dwelling, and the new erection looks little fitted to afford them an asylum.

Rounding the foot of Barrow Head, in which traces of iron ore are distinctly visible, and attempts to win it still more so, and in which copper ore has also been found, we open into a bay, at the extremity of which stands the Wyke. This is a farm-house, whose name describes its position, as Wyke signifies a bay with a low shore. For instance, there is a Pullwyke Bay in Windermere, and in Derwent Water, Sandwyke, &c. To the south-east of this farm lies Humphrey Head, which, limestone like, has its slope to the north, wooded with almost impenetrable hazel, while to the south-west it rises perpendicularly from the sand.

As the route over the isthmus of the promontory is rugged, if the tide have retreated, it is best to proceed direct from Kent's Bank to Humphrey Head. By this way we participate a little in the feeling which this desert of sand imparts. The objects at a distance appear distorted,—sometimes magnified, and at other times sailing, as it were, on a line of water. In some states of the atmosphere, the mirage appearances of the east present themselves, and shadowy lands and woods magically spring up

D

on the barren waste. These are pictures from the shore reflected on the vapour which arises from the wet sand. Sometimes a dense mist prevents the traveller seeing beyond a few yards around him, and it is wonderful how the drivers of the daily coaches find their way on such occasions. Perhaps evening has come on, and adds to the gloom. The tide has washed out the track. The leaders' heads are felt, not seen. A few yards' error may pitch the coach, when crossing the waters of the channel, into a deep gulf made by the shifting sand. Fearlessly, but carefully, the coachman proceeds, while his faithful team seem instinctively to hasten to their journey's end. Sitting by his side, the box passenger begins to feel nervous ; but, as there is no timidity in his neighbour, he turns to the driver,—" Coachee, how do you know the road ? No danger, hei-heigh ?"—" No, sur, no danger in general. We drives by the wind, sur, in the mist and the dark."— "By the wind!" says the southern.—" Yes, sur, by the wind. I feels which side of the face it takes as I leaves the shore. I knows as how it does not change much, and I keep the cheek just to the quarter which will land us safe. It is all one, sur, day or night, when the wind keeps the compass to the point ; but when there's no wind, and the mist is thick, why we do as we can, sur." The traveller puts this down in his note book ; and let all tourists who climb hills without a compass, remember that the wind is the shepherd's needle, and by it he steers on the edge of precipices and through bogs when the pathway is unseen a yard a-head.

In passing over the sand, the reflecting mind observes an additional proof of the prolific character of creation. Besides the numerous travellers and pedestrians crossing

from Ulverston to Lancaster, he observes, at every little
wash of water, the nets of fishermen, fixed on stakes about
two feet high, and forming a long circle which the tide
raises as it flows, allowing the fish to pass under. As it
recedes, the current bears the net down close to the sand,
and, when the tide has gone out, the fisherman, by his
hands and feet, discovers flooks, plaice, and sometimes
salmon, in the little pools of water above the nets. Winter and summer, daylight and starlight, in wet and in fair,
these poor fellows go down to the bleak sands, to look
after their nets. Two villages, Flookburgh and Allithwaite, are chiefly supported by fishing and " cockling."
The latter employs the children, wives, and young women
of the fishermen's families. These people follow each
receding tide, and on the banks of sand, called " cockle
skeers," find the cockles. A small mark on the sand,
unnoticed by the stranger, but understood by the ex-
perienced eye, indicates where the shell-fish has buried
itself,—and the cockler, with a three-pronged instrument
bent at the extremity of the prongs, scrapes up the fish
with astonishing rapidity.

A friend of our's, who once saw a barn full of these
people on a winter's evening, has described the scene as
very striking. Women bronzed to a copper hue—little
ragged children with hair as rough and of the colour of the
ass's hide—strong muscular-looking young women drench-
ed with wet, were all crowded together with their baskets,
just as they had come off their work. They were mea-
suring their lots to the dealer, who is commissioned to
take them in his cart to the market ; and these eagerly
vociferating people, their features lit up with a few far-
thing candles, would have made an admirable picture for

Teniers. It is said that, from the sands at Rampside and Hest Bank, as many as eighteen tons weight of cockles have been sent in a week to Preston and Manchester. The cocklers, like all those who follow exposed pursuits, are rough and unpolished, and, in this age of universal benevolence, they deserve the sympathy and aid of the upper classes, for their long hours and want of home comforts. They are not, however, dissolute. It is said they durst not quarrel on the sands, lest they should drive off (as their superstition says they would) the whole of the cockles for the season.

It is a mile from Kent's Bank to Humphrey Head, and on turning the point of the promontory, there rises up a sublime cliff—here whitened by exposure—there covered with short shrubs and heath—again it is towering like the battlement of a Titanic stronghold—then, again, it is covered with a deep rich velvet hanging of noble and venerable yew trees, which almost adhere to its sides. At its highest point a vast cavity yawns open, out of which you imagine that the giant owner of the fortress ought to appear. But the natives of the district have surrendered it to fairies, for whom it is said to be a home. Whatever doubt may hang over the existence of these inmates, there is no doubt of one species, for the re-echoed cawing of the jack-daws peoples the cliff with an interminable voice.

Underneath this cavern there flows out of the bowels of the rock a mineral water, famous for its medicinal virtues, and which, from time immemorial, has been denominated the Holy Well.

To it, for some years, quite a regiment of miners from Alston, in Cumberland, used to resort. They rode all the way on little mountain " galloways," quartered themselves in the neighbouring villages, bathed in the sea, and drank the waters in quantity,—a gallon per diem sometimes,— and went back renewed and invigorated. Some came annually for forty years. The bad state of the mining trade, and the discovery of mineral waters in their own neighbourhood, have, of late, prevented this annual migration. If the tide of fashion could be turned, and the visitors who crowd to the foreign spas could be drawn to the Holy Well, they would find its waters as medicinal, its air as pure, and its sources of enjoyment infinitely more beautiful than two-thirds of the crowded Badens of Germany.

The well and adjoining land is the property of Mr. George Gelderd, of Aikrigg End, near Kendal, who allows visitors to ramble over the promontory, whence the views are delightful, though not so extensive as from Hampsfield Fell. From the former the Isle of Man may be seen; from the latter Ireland and Wales are visible in favourable weather. The rare plants which are found upon Humphrey Head attract the footsteps of the enterprising botanist. Many years ago the cottage adjoining the well was inhabited by a fisherman's numerous family, who lived on the first floor, under which, in a dark black-looking kitchen, there was a small iron boiler, filled with spa water, and heated by turf. Sometimes the ancient dame in attendance—the mother of two generations at least—used a black cauldron, upon a hearth fire, instead of the boiler. Then with her dark countenance in that gloomy apartment, her dishevelled locks floating over her disordered attire, she looked like a witch of former days, dispensing her potions to twenty or thirty horsemen crowding round her dirty door. She had stores of tales for the visitor, and though too unreal and too wild for the present period, they illustrate those legendary marvels, whose existence is rapidly decaying in this part. When narrating a history, she sat down on a three-legged stool, by the embers of the hearth fire, wearing a linsey-woolsey lower garment, and a semi kind of gown, reaching only to the hips, with short wide sleeves, which left bare her once muscular, though now shrivelled, arms, one of which she leaned a kimbo on her knee. In her right hand she held a tobacco pipe, of about four inches long, and black with forty years' usage, and which she smoked vehemently at every short interval of her tale. The one window was in a corner,— its few panes nearly all stuffed with rags,—but a gleam or two from the burning turf would occasionally irradiate this almost dark apartment, and render the gloom more visible. Old Rachael is now gathered to her forefathers, her family is dispersed, the miners are seldom seen, the key of the well must now be sought at a neighbouring farm-house, and the visitor must luxuriate alone in abundant doses of the waters in all the romantic and wild solitariness of this interesting scene.

Near to Humphrey Head there is a very attractive ramble, which the visitor may enjoy by taking the road to Allithwaite until it is intercepted by the Kent's Bank road, which he must pursue for a short distance, until he can turn to the right into a large enclosure, and so ascend to Barrow's summer-house, where an extensive prospect on all sides awaits him. To the west is seen Allithwaite, picturesquely situated in a sheltered hollow. Flookburgh is in the distance, and the more extended view includes many of the objects which we have before described as visible from neighbouring heights.

The wide-spread plain of rich land to the south-west

attracts the attention of the observer, and he learns, with surprise, that hundreds of acres of most fruitful soil, and which is now burdened with plenteous crops, have been stolen from the dominion of the sea. At the high tides he may stand upon the bank which protects the reclaimed land,—up which wave after wave rolls with threatening breakers, while, on the other side of the bank or dyke, the husbandman, considerably below the level of the water, gets his hay, or reaps his corn, in safety. Valve gates are used for the land streams, and the shutters in the arches of the bridges are closed by the flowing tide, and effectually prevent its ingress to the reclaimed fields. Several years since the tide broke through the barrier, and threatened destruction to the farmer and his crops. Much damage was done, but strenuous exertions limited the extent of the injury. These Holland-like works were principally accomplished by the enterprize of the late Mr. Towers, of Duddon Grove, and Mr. Stockdale, of Cark. At the base of the hill on which the observer stands, he will not fail to notice the grey tower of an old fortified mansion which is now a farm-house, and the Peel used for the storage of hay and as a byre for cows.

This crumbling specimen of the habitations of an ancient race is well worthy a visit, and is reached by descending from Barrow's summer-house through Allithwaite, and along some shady lanes, where the fragrant honeysuckle pours a most delicious perfume, and seems to intertwine among the hazel, the thorn, and the bramble, in a continuous wreath, bearing a remarkable profusion of odoriferous flowers.

Wraysholme Tower stands in a low flat situation, and, with Winder Hall, formerly guarded this arm of Morecambe Bay. It was for many years the residence of the chief branch of the Harringtons, who held large possessions in this neighbourhood, and who obtained considerable accessions of property at the time of the Norman Conquest. Aldingham, the once flourishing Saxon town, whose very site has been washed away by the sea, belonged to them in the year 1346. But it is probable, as Aldingham was acquired by marriage from the Flemings, and left the Harringtons in the same manner, that Wraysholme continued their chief abode at the time of their greatest prosperity.

CHAPTER V.

FLOOKBURGH AND HOLKER HALL.

HOLKER HALL

CHAPTER V.

In this era of thought—expansive, noble thought—pene-trating by new and untrodden paths into the regions of science and practical truth, there is a danger of age be-coming disregarded, and the past looked upon as utterly degenerate. Some superficial people already speak of age as a shadow, and of antiquity as a byword ; but, with the true philosopher, age is another name for experience, and that which has stood the test of time has the witness in itself that it was adapted for the years in which it arose, and, to a greater or less degree, fulfilled its destinies during the period of its existence.

The aristocracy of this country may attribute the prin-cipal portion of the obloquy with which they have been assailed to the spirit of aggrandisement prevalent in many of their order, or to the dissolute and immoral character of others who usurp the distinction of peers of the realm. When the world can point to a titled family distinguished alike by its honor, respectability, and benevolence, the coronet becomes dignified by the wearers, and public suf-frage acknowledges the worth of so true a nobility.

In a secluded portion of the county of Lancaster, totally different from what the distant reader pictures the smoky manufacturing Lancashire to be, there stands, in an ancient park, the mansion of a noble family, whose unblemished integrity and dignified affability have, for many years, approved the existence of an aristocracy—like-minded—to the consciences of all observers.

Holker Hall, in the parish of Cartmel, is about three miles from Grange. It is not so ancient as many of the residences of the old Saxon families in Cartmel and Furness, the earliest memorials of its existence going no further back than the middle of the 16th century, when it was the property of Christopher Preston, the second son of Sir Thomas Preston, of Preston Patrick, in Westmorland.

The Prestons were an ancient family residing at Preston Patrick at the time of the conquest. Soon after that event, Preston *Richard* was the possession of a Richard de Preston successively for the space of two hundred years, and hence its distinctive name is derived.

Preston *Patrick* was granted by Gilbert Fitz Reinfred to Gospatrick, whose grandson, Patrick, " son of Thomas son of Gospatrick," had the grant confirmed by William de Lancaster. The Curwen family, in Cumberland, trace their descent from Patricius de Culwen, to whom Preston Patrick belonged. Thus there is in the family name of Patrick a corresponding clue to the name Preston *Patrick*.

About the year 1685, Catharine Preston, to whom the property at Holker had descended, married Sir William Lowther, of Marsk, in Yorkshire. Although Marsk is also situated near to the sea coast, at the foot of the Cleveland Hills, and in a pleasing locality, there was no hesitation on the part of this branch of the Lowthers in adopting the much more attractive Holker as their residence, which it continued to be until the year 1756, when Sir William Lowther dying unmarried, left his estates in Holker and Furness to his cousin, Lord George Augustus Cavendish, the ancestor of the present owner, the Earl of Burlington, who resides here several months in each year, and who has recently completed extensive alterations, so as entirely to change the architectural appearance of the building.

To the connoiseur in the fine arts there are many attractions in the valuable collection of paintings possessed by the Earl, which he generously allows to be opened to the visitor.

Having heard much of the interesting character of the place, we set out one fine morning, and, after a pleasant ride through Allithwaite and Flookburgh, we came in sight of the peculiarly rounded and flowing outline of the Holker woods.

Flookburgh is a long continuous street of humble houses, occupied by fishermen and a few farmers. It possesses a large chapel of remarkably plain external appearance, bearing little resemblance to the matron church at Cartmel. There are also two comfortable inns, where visitors who come to bathe and to drink the Holywell water may be accommodated.

If appears once to have been a more important place, having been, as its name imports, a market borough. The market was held by a charter granted to the Prior of Cartmel by Edward the First : subsequent to the dissolution of the religious houses it was removed to Cartmel. Adjoining the village there stands a very extensive range of buildings, intended for farm accommodation, and arranged so as to comprise every convenience on a large scale. The *only* deficiency is the entire want of produce and of stock for such a convenient place, and which the builder can scarcely have contemplated! We were told that these buildings had been nearly unoccupied for many years.

Proceeding to the village of Cark, we find another vast pile of building erected for a cotton mill, but wholly unoccupied, and now fast going to decay. Leaving to our left the excellent mansion of Mr. Stockdale, and to our right the interesting residence of the old family of Rawlinson, Cark Hall, we entered Holker, and were attracted by the neat cottages and village school, whose flower gardens indicated the fostering care of the owners of the Hall, which stands a very short distance within the entrance gates.

A sudden turn in the carriage drive brought us unexpectedly close to the house, immediately opposite to the gothic entrance. As the interior of the house and the paintings would require further detail than is consistent with this paper, it must suffice to say, that the works of art which grace the apartments are well worthy the attention of the visitor. Having been delighted with the internal decorations of the house, and irresistibly attracted by the lovely scenes outside the windows, from the library we stepped on to a terrace overlooking a parterre of flower-beds, planted with a uniformity in accordance with the architecture of the building. Passing on to what might be called an American flower-garden, we revelled in the luxuriance of rare and fragrant blossoms, which crowded every bed, all so tastefully disposed and in such perfect arrangement, that the natural beauty of each variety was enhanced by the judicious manner in which it was contrasted with those which surrounded it.

Azaleas, in rich profusion, from the pale blush to the brightest orange and most brilliant scarlet ; beds of rhododendrons of gigantic growth, which transported us in idea to a far more southern clime ; varieties of native heaths, nurtured until they had attained a noble size; and not least welcome, the sweet odour of the fragrant daphne, would not allow us to pass its unobtrusive flowers without admiring them, amidst the blaze of glowing beauty.

This charming garden is so arranged as to present a constant succession of flowers throughout the summer, whilst the luxuriant evergreens clothe it with a mantle of beauty even in winter's stormiest day, almost bringing back the perception of summer's attractiveness amid the desolation of the year.

We threw ourselves beneath the shade of some magnificent Portugal laurels, close to the basin of a fountain where the gold and silver fish darted beneath the sunbeams, which were reflected by their glossy scales with prismatic hues.

Here we commanded a view of the Hall. Its mixed style of architecture might with some awaken criticism. From others the Tudor Gothic would meet with but little favour. Let those better skilled in such matters decide. For ourselves, we passed under the shade of noble lime trees, about whose beauty no critics could contend, and near to the remains of a once-magnificent Cedar of Lebanon, now scathed by lightning, but seeming, amidst its ruins, to claim the respect due to dignified age. We then opened upon another garden, which spread itself suddenly before us, hanging in terraces on the slope of a hill, and surrounded on every side by towering forest trees, among which openings had been made, displaying glades of smooth green turf, upon which the bright sunlight glanced and flickered as the breeze stirred the bending foliage.

This second garden is evidently a new creation—a spot won from the forest like the progress of the new world—ancient nature retreating before the necessities and luxuries of man.

Beds of roses, on a magnificent scale, are spread on the level platform of this conquered ground, and festoons of climbing roses are flung from bed to bed with a wild beauty, which, when they are in full bloom, give a most festive air to the scene. Stately pines, in the full perfection of their early growth, contrast well with those flowery wreaths among which they stand interspersed, like mentors amid groups of sportive children.

Stone steps, ornamented with vases, lead from terrace to terrace. On the highest a pretty conservatory is filled with tender flowers from climes yet more favoured than this deliciously sheltered spot.

Winding walks lead into the recesses of the wood, and seats of various forms tempted us to rest. We thought of the fair being who, a few years since, graced these grounds, her radiant smiles bespeaking the benignant affections of her heart. We had heard from the villagers much of her humility and benevolence, and we communed of her self-denial which led her to walk to the distant house of prayer, rather than derange the Sabbath quiet of her domestics, at a time when her delicacy required every consideration. We recalled the heartfelt gratitude and affectionate veneration with which all spoke of her worth, and the delighted "good morning," or "good evening," with which the numerous sinecure pensioners who are employed in the park respectfully greeted the Lady of the Hall, and received, in return, the kind inquiries of that amiable peeress. Born of a noble and ancient lineage— allied to house as noble and as ancient—the mother of the heir of a princely inheritance, with all the comforts that the fondest and faithfulest affection, combined with boundless wealth, could bestow—unspoiled by flattery or prosperity, she lived for the benefit of others, and to His praise whose self-denying example she sought to follow. The blessing of them who were ready to perish rested oftentimes upon her spirit, and, falling asleep in Jesus, she winged her flight to a holier world.

A visit to Holker ought not to be a hurried one. Time should be allowed to sit beneath the spreading oaks, to listen to the thousand tones of nature in a summer's morning—insects crowding the air with their multitudinous voices—the bustling humble bee resounding his musical violin amidst the smaller notes of the minute winged tribes, and the verdure at your feet sending up a low murmur of living animation. The skylark pours down upon you his thrilling tones from his floating pinnacle, and each branch amid the sheltering foliage contributes a songster, to make up the melody of one vast universal hymn of praise and joy.

When at noon these voices were hushed into silence, the deep repose of nature filled the mind with meditative feelings. Not a creature besides was in the gardens, and while the gentle breeze whispered soft music in the branches above our head, we sought to imprint upon our memory the pictures of beauty around us, so as to recal their living reality at some future time, when the weary soul should seek relief amid the cares and bustle of the world.

After having explored the garden, the region of flowers, and the lovely "pleasaunce" which they adorn, we followed the carriage drives in the park until we reached some rising ground, whence, with the park at our feet, we commanded an extensive prospect over the Ulverston bay.

The undulating ground and the graceful groups of trees form an infinity of sweet landscapes, which cannot fail to kindle any latent spark of artist feeling. The view of the estuary, with its broken coast line, recessed into minor bays, wooded rocks rising precipitously from the land, or by low thickly wooded grounds stretching out to the sea-beach, is extremely pleasing. Evergreens and flowering shrubs grow in profusion and great luxuriance. The mild sea breeze seems to be favourable to them, and more healthy and vigorous evergreens are not to be found anywhere in England, unless in some parts of Devonshire or Cornwall.

Conishead Priory, the Bardsea shipping, and Birkrigg, present themselves across the bay, and the prettily wooded Chapel Island, with its ruined Chapel, breaks the view by the admirable foreshortening effect—if we may be allowed to use the term—which it produces. The little religious house on the island was maintained by the monks of Conishead, one or two of the fraternity doing duty there. Tradition describes its purpose to be the meeting in prayer with the travellers who cross the bay. If so, it is an evidence of the constant reference to religion which characterized the middle ages, but whether always as spiritual as desirable, it is not the province of this paper to discuss.

The Park at Holker is not very extensive, but the wooded heights behind it, in which bridle-roads are constructed for many miles in length, afford every facility for riding through a picturesque country, commanding views of Leven Water and the mountains at the head of Windermere, as well as a most lovely peep into Thurston vale, with the magnificent range of the Coniston hills in the back-ground.

These woods extend to a domain which is very ancient in its traditionary memorials, and which is most attractively situated. Bigland Hall, and the family which resides there, must look back, through an uninterrupted succession, to a Saxon ancestry, who covered with the grain which has given it its name, the land they won by their rude husbandry from the wild forest which surrounded it.

Holker affords much gratification to the guests at the Hall in the shooting season. The game on the property is preserved without difficulty, the race of poachers not being so desperate as in other northern districts.

The number of the birds astonishes the casual visitor, and their tameness is not much surpassed by the poultry in the admirable range of farm-buildings recently erected by the Earl.

We took leave of this charming spot, breathing the wish that it may long be possessed by worthy descendants of the present honoured race; and by a lovely road through the woods and across the park, which once formed a part of the Cartmel Priory grounds, we reached the main road, and turned our steps homewards.

CHAPTER VI.

LINDALE AND CASTLEHEAD.

NEWBY BRIDGE

CHAPTER VI.

WHILE the objects to the south of Grange are replete with interest, there are others to the north well worthy of admiration.

Let us bend our steps towards Lindale. After passing the farm-house at the foot of the hill, we gradually ascend a spur of the Eggerslack range of rocks. This spur, or shoulder, hides its termination in the sand on the shore. Half way up its luxuriant bank, and in a recess made by its curved form, stands Blawith, the residence of the relict of the late Thomas Holme Maude, Esq., which may be said to repose upon the breast of a semi-crescent hill. It is em-bosomed among flowers and evergreen shrubs, having, for a fine back-ground, a rocky range crowned with larches and oaks. This range encircles it in its protecting arms, and shelters it from the north, the west, and the north-east winds.

In front is a grassy slope, which is partially girdled by a minor wooded ridge. Nature has so sheltered this lovely spot, that the breath of heaven can scarcely approach it with aught but the balmy airs of the south, while the warm and cheerful rays of the sun can bask upon the bright green verdure of the hollowed lawn, or sparkle in the waters of the small stream which winds around its base.

Over this slope, and to the south, the view towards the bay is calm and beautiful.

It can be no surprise that in this warm locality,—and at Blawith, the most sheltered situation it possesses,—there should flourish plants and flowers, which, in other situations, require stoves and the carefulest cultivation.

The building is a commodious and genteel residence, not large, but embracing all needful conveniences for the elegancies of life. The delicate health of the lady of the mansion prevents its being accessible to visitors, in the way which her charitable and kindly disposition would have allowed. At certain seasons, however, when the flock of school children whom she educates meet to receive rewards and gifts in clothing, this regulation is partially relaxed, and the grounds exhibit a cheerful and animated picture.

The walks in the woods are extensive, and the feathered tribes carefully protected. No one can have dwelt at Grange without luxuriating, morning and evening, in the delicious tones of the blackbirds, thrushes, and other birds which give life to the Blawith and Yewbarrow plantations.

Here, as has been before observed of this locality in general, the woods and lanes are a prolific field for the entomologist. During one of our rambles we were attracted by the merry voices of children, and we turned aside from the sea-shore through a gate near some coppice, and found a lady, with four happy children, in a sweet shady glade in the Blawith grounds, that glistened

GRANGE FROM BLAWITH MEADOW

with wild flowers, studying natural history at one of the largest ant hills we had ever seen. It was conical in construction, nearly two feet high, with a rounded summit, and two to three feet wide at the base. Countless ants were busy exposing and turning the eggs in the sun. Numbers were departing or returning from their expeditions of forage for food, each as intently occupied with his work as if the fate of empires rested upon it. The little naturalists, with earnest interest, were watching the active artificers. One little open-faced boy, of seven years, was kneeling on the ground criticising the dissection of a dead beetle which he had found and placed in one of the roads to the insect city, and which had at once been seized upon by the outward bound purveyors for stores. One detachment of ants was severing the wings, and others bearing fragments of the body to the hill. The apparent weights which they removed made the little fellow marvel. A laughing little rosy-faced girl of five, was exultingly bringing wild strawberries gathered on the shore : she added them to others which had been thrown upon the hill, giving the storekeepers of the cells occupation in cutting them into portable pieces, and carefully taking them down into the interior of the hill. The eldest child, a thoughtful-looking girl of ten, had brought some sugar from home, and was attentively noticing on which ants it devolved to garner up this dainty food. Many passed it with indifference, having other divisions of labour to attend to ; but the purveyors speedily removed it to their " cupboards," to use the little girl's expression, as she archly looked up. A fourth child, a little damsel of eight years, with a pale but animated face, full of elasticity of voice and manner, bearing in her hands crumbs of bread and a dead fly, contrasted with the quiet studiousness of her brother and sister. She ran from one to the other, exclaiming, " Here is an ant with wings just alighted on the ground. See, see, he is gnawing them off! He has found a home here, I suppose. There, I have given some crumbs to the bakers, and the dead fly to the butchers, and they are using might and main to carry them to their shelves and larders ;" and then, placing a fir-apple on the hill, " now, ants," she said, "turn out the sweepers and cleaners, to get this intruder out of the way. Look, the store-keepers don't mind it; but here are some ants carefully mounting it, and going all over it, to see the size, I suppose, and examine what it is! Are they engineers ?" she said, turning to the lady. " Sappers and miners, I presume," was the smiling reply, "employed by this little commonwealth to remove nuisances,—you had better save them the trouble by removing it yourself."

Truly, an ant hill is an interesting sight. Solomon commends it to the attention of the sluggard, but surely the industrious man also may learn from it lessons of wisdom, prudence, and zeal, which he would do well to follow.

With such reflections we left the little students to pursue their investigations into the habits and economy of this insect community, pleased with the thought that they were thus storing up knowledge for future happiness and usefulness. Little did we suppose that, in a few short weeks, two of this lively and animated group would be called from the pleasures and pursuits of earth, to share the better and holier joys of Heaven.

The name Blawith seems to be of British origin, but what its signification may be is not very clear.

Leaving this pleasing spot to the right, we attain, by the high road, the summit of the rising ground, and open out upon a beautiful panoramic view, looking far into the vale of Kendal, with the most inland reaches of Morecambe Bay in the foreground.

On reaching Lindale, the picturesque situation of the little church attracts admiration. The village is built upon the two sides of a small glen, or mountain gorge, formed by the course of a rapid streamlet which is used for turning a corn-mill, and whose mill-dam, or the fall of the water over the weir, which, in Scotland, is denominated a " linn," probably gave the name to the village. The humble cottages are located without any reference to order or design, and look as if washed into their places by the turbulence of some vast overflow of the torrent, rather than by the hand of the architect ; and yet there is a picturesque effect given to the village by this irregularity, which the lovers of the rustic must infinitely prefer to the straight uniformity of contract-built streets.

Towards the head of the gorge stands the church, half hid among trees, but its gothic tower lifts its white turrets with tasteful beauty from their verdant foliage. It is a neat and simple structure, and must be a boon to the neighbourhood. Its pious minister has many hearers from among the visitors at Grange, notwithstanding my hostess's predilections for the more pretending edifice at Cartmel.

Further up the glen, and in a basin-like portion of it, there has been created, within a few years, a most lovely spot. Its site was almost barren when George Webster, Esq. commenced the erection of his country villa, near the abode of his forefathers, and, by beautiful arrangements, availed himself of the capabilities of the situation, adding ornamental planting, and forming artificial pieces of water, so as to elicit from the rugged rocks around the ancient dwelling more beauties than nature dreamt of for that locality, and the combinations of art and natural scenery with near and distant prospects, have rendered Eller How an abode which may be long sought for elsewhere, but in vain.

Before returning from the neighbourhood of Lindale, a visit should be paid to Castle Head. It is situated at the foot of the range on which Lindale is placed. The house is not remarkable in any way, and remains unoccupied. The grounds immediately around the house are pleasant, but the great object of interest is a towering rock, almost conical, which stands completely isolated from the neighbouring hills, and must have been severed by some grand convulsion of nature. It is a limestone rock, and has been the origin of the name, having been called Castle Head long before the erection of the residence.

By some persons the term has been interpreted "Castle Stead," and has been deemed conclusive of the place having been used as a castle by the Romans. Of this we have no traces. It is not, apparently, in the proximity of their roads, neither is the situation such as they were accustomed to select for their military stations.

Its present appropriation, without any antiquarian reminiscences, is quite sufficient to attract the curious. It is ascended by a spiral pathway, which gradually takes the visitor from the rich umbrageous foliage of the lawn to the lofty summit whence the eye reaches all over the bay. The pathway is partially excavated, and partially sustained by masonry. The hill is wooded, and the view to the north commands a lovely peep inland. Terraces are formed at convenient positions in the ascent, and you first find

F. Webster delin.

C. Huttmann Lithog. Liverpool.

ELLER HOW.

yourself surveying the southern prospect of lake-like bay,
and a little further you open out upon a wholly different
region of hill and scar and woodland. Another circle, and
again and again this is repeated. Each time ascending
higher, the view becomes amplified, and fresh objects greet
the eye. The pathways are beautifully designed. A
strawberry bank sometimes tempts the weary one, and he
reposes behind evergreens which shut him out from the
world, and produce the feeling of seclusion on this lofty
pinnacle. Elsewhere he starts back, as the walk follows
the ledge of a beetling precipice, near the foot of which
the tide dashes, when at the highest. Not far off is an
arbour, where the poet or the solitary may indulge in a
contemplative mood, hanging on a tree seat, suspended,
as it were, from the very verge of the topmost brow.

It is difficult to describe this romantic place, and more
so, because were we to represent the character of the lovely
views which are beheld from the crest of this lofty rock-
tower, we should recall many of the names which are now
familiar to our readers. The giant scar of Whitbarrow is,
however, more effectually seen as an object of beauty from
this point than from anywhere else near Grange.

Besides these walks, other vistitors may find at Castle
Head an object of interest in the mausoleum of one of its
owners. We saw it last after our descent from the rock,
and we rejoice that we did not visit it before ascending,
for the dark death-like sepulchral spot chilled our blood,
and made us long for some sunlight, which we quickly
obtained in our walk back by the sands to our peaceful
cottage at Grange.

Castle Head is the property of R. Wright, Esq. of Child-
wall, near Liverpool, who appropriates the marsh land

to the rearing of horses, and we were told that considerable celebrity has been attached to some of those which have been sold from his farm.

In our return, we were attracted to extend our walk by Meathop point, which is a fine cliff of minor magnitude, and crowned with picturesque larches. It forms a breakwater for the channel of the Kent, whose versatile course is sometimes at one side and sometimes at the other. Occasionally it washes deep with its dark waters the foot of Meathop Crag, and it would, were it not for this barrier, flow over the adjoining land. Arnside Point on the east, and Meathop on the west, influence the course of the waters down the bay.

Appendix to Chapter vi.

CARTMEL SANDS

APPENDIX TO CHAPTER VI.

Since the publication of this chapter, our attention has been drawn by an antiquarian acquaintance to the omission of any explanation of the name of Meathop, or Meathorp. We are informed that the term Meath is the British word for a place of residence, or a dwelling, and that Thorp is the Saxon addition, signifying a house and its adjoining tenements. In this we entirely agree, because the "Dorp" of Jutland and Saxony has, in this country, almost universally assumed the orthography of Thorpe, and is very prevalent in Yorkshire. It is no unusual thing to find, in the names of places, a repetition of signification in two languages, on occasions where a country has been colonized, or conquered by successive races. Thus Englishmen have, in America, added the term "river," or "mount," or "land," to the native name which includes, in its signification, these respective characteristics.

It was quite natural for our Saxon ancestors to add their own termination "Thorp" or "the dwellings" at Meath, to the word Meath, which they found to be the British name of the place. A singularly interesting elucidation of this mode of explanatory nomenclature occurs in the name of a small village in Cumberland.

Torpenhow derives the different syllables of which it is compounded from words all similarly descriptive of its position. "Pen" being the British term for a hill, or rising ground, was found by the Saxons; they added the term "How," which, in Teutonic, has the same signification. The Scandinavian invaders brought from the east the word "Tor," whose meaning—an eminence—is alike on the plains of Asia, the centre of Europe, and the shores of our own island. In each language the situation of Torpenhow is accurately described. By some the term Tor has been traced to Thor, one of the Saxon gods, and it is not improbable that Torpenhow has been in succession a place for idolatrous worship; but that Tor, signifying a hill, was the proximate cause of the adjunct, there can be little doubt. Many similar cases occur in the names of places on *the coast* of England, while the word Thor, when introduced, as it frequently is, almost always retains the aspirate letter, and is found in the *interior* of the island. That originally the signification of Tor has been derived from the wooded hill or grove on which Thor was worshipped in regions far east, is not improbable, but it is clear that Tor had become an incorporated word in the language, and of general signification, when used in the name to which we have alluded.

While agreeing with our acquaintance in the explanation of the word Meathorp, we do not concur with him in his analysis of the name of the adjoining place, Milnthorpe. Of the latter syllable, Thorpe, in this case also there can be no doubt but the former syllable can scarcely be traced, as he suggests, to the Saxon word " Meol," signifying a cape, or flat, or bare land near the shore, and which is incorporated in the names Millum, Meolholme, Milford, &c. &c. It seems more natural to trace Milnthorpe to " the village adjoining the mill," especially as the same word is found at Milthorp, near Sedbergh, and at Milness, near Crooklands, both away from the sea.

In the same chapter we had hesitated about the signification of the name Blawith. We have been reminded that the pronunciation is similar to the British word Blaidd, signifying a wolf. It is very probable that this word enters into the composition of Blawith, and that, by the Saxons, "Thwaite," or Wolffield, had been the origin of the word, shortened by the abbreviating process of usage, from Blaidthwaite to Blawith. But we do not see it very clearly. We have also been told that instead of tracing the meaning of the word Lindale to the remains of the British tongue in Scotland, we should have gone directly to the ancient word "lyn," which, in British, signifies a pool, and hence that the mill-dam at Lindale, and not the weir, is the origin of the name. We admit the correctness of these remarks; at the same time it must be remembered, that Scotland being for many years predominant in northern England, and the south of Scotland being the home of the Britons, it is easier to trace the adaptation of the term through their tongue.

CHAPTER VII.

THE SAND.—CHAPEL ISLAND.—FURNESS.—RAMPSIDE
PIEL CASTLE.

FURNESS ABBEY

CHAPTER VII.

WE should very imperfectly perform the duties of a
" Guide to Grange," if we omitted to notice some of the
more distant places of interest included in the district
which the topographer calls "Plain Furness," and the
local tongue denominates "Low Furness." We would
gladly point the way to this truly interesting district, and
trust that a slight sketch of a pleasant excursion thither,
may tempt others to follow our example. Our primary
aim was to reach an object conspicuous in every distant
prospect from Grange.

We had often pictured what a nearer view of Piel Castle
would show us, and at last we resolved to explore that
" hoary pile," which is the subject of Wordsworth's beautiful elegiac stanzas, and whose weather-beaten but lordly
remains are gradually crumbling away, upon a small island
at the very extremity of the promontory which forms the
north-western boundary of Morecambe Bay.

Summer's brightest sunrise tipped the summit of Ingleborough with its roseate hue, when we started to cross
the Ulverston sands, that being the nearest way to Piel.
We had been half tempted to take a boat, and visit by sea
the Pile of Fouldrey (as the castle is sometimes called),

G

especially as a young seafaring friend had discovered a skilful boatman well acquainted with the peculiar navigation of the bay, and whose skiff, he said, cut the dancing ripple of the tide " like a thing of life."

He described the scene from the water as peculiarly beautiful,—the mountains at the head of the bay as dappled with the wandering shadows of the awakening clouds, —the morning beams as piercing the recesses of the rugged hills,—and the mists as creeping up their lofty pinnacles, crowning some with impenetrable mystery, and circling others with a diadem of silvery glory.

Unpersuaded by his glowing description, we induced him to join our party, and mounting the vehicle already described—" a shandry cart"—we jogged along till we reached Cark, where we entered upon the sands.

Holker Hall, to the right, was seen amid its sheltering woods, and when the view opened out beyond Park Head we were perfectly enchanted.

We rode on until, in the centre of the vast plain, every object on the shore, touching the sand, seemed to have a watery mistiness before it, but above this all was clear. The mountains of Conistone and Windermere, and the rich green of the valley of the Crake, were blushing with a vermilion glow. We were the first who had crossed that morning. The former tracks were all washed out by the tide, and nothing but a few furze bushes, placed here and there, called " broggs," served to shew the direction we ought to take. The sand was hard and firm, and we travelled on in silence. Not a sound was to be heard, for our vehicle moved noiselessly, and we felt the solitariness of the wide waste by which we were surrounded, girdled though it was by a panorama of beauty.

We had arranged to visit Chapel Island on our way, the crossing of the channel permitting us to do so. This island is a limestone rock, standing much above the level of the highest tides. To the south the rocks are cut abruptly by the flowing tide: to the north-east the approach is by a gradual beach-like acclivity. It is truly a verdant spot. The trees do not grow to a great height, but the brambles, underwood, and long grass show how rich the soil is, produced by the decomposition of the rock, the wind-borne sand, and the deposit of salt, in the course of ages. The chapel has been a small, but complete edifice, the remains of its ruined windows and the old door-way tell of the early times in which it was erected. Situated opposite to Conishead Priory, the canons of St· Augustine delighted in its quiet seclusion, where, cut off from the world, they could exercise their devotional duties and pursue their contemplative studies. There, also, the sailors attached to the barques which visited Furness, could perform worship, and make their votive offerings for their safe voyages. The traveller who had accomplished the adventurous crossing of the estuaries from Lancaster, —the difficulties of which the Roman general, Agricola, encountered, and thought them worthy to be communicated by himself to the historian Tacitus,—was happy to reach the oratory of Chapel Island, to return thanks-givings for his escape from so many dangers, or there he said his *Ave Maria* for protection, before he entered upon this formidable undertaking. There was an hospice also, and the black canons were not only ready to give the tra-veller spiritual counsel, but an official lay member of the Priory was, like the good monks of St. Bernard in the mountains of Switzerland, prepared to guide and assist him across the treacherous waste. Here we remained while the tide flowed, and had time to contemplate the view which the high water rendered even more beautiful. The bay resembled a vast lake, whose shores were infinitely varied both in outline and colour ; here, the emerald verdure was deepened into an intensity of shade, while, beyond, it faded away till the shadowy tints melted into the soft grey of the distant hills. Above us was the bright blue dome of heaven, whose hue was reflected in the waters, rippling and curling their foam-crested waves before a pleasant breeze. The island is now inhabited by a fisherman and his wife, at the instance of the owner of the Priory, who has erected a cottage close to the ruins. It is chiefly visited by parties of pleasure, whose pic-nics form a strange contrast to the pursuits of the solitary devotees who formerly occupied it.

When the tide receded we resumed our expedition. On nearing some rocks we came to a hollow in the sand, which, by the way, is far from level ; and at the other side of the hollow we saw the channel, which had recently approached nearer to the Ulverston shore, and in its sidelong course, had formed the basin we were to cross. It was still cutting abruptly into one bank, here and there only leaving a sloping acclivity, up one of which we were to ascend.

" In truth, yon is a queer looking craft," suddenly said our seafaring companion, as he pointed to an undescribable black object in the water. We pronounced it to be a porpoise ; he termed it a Norwegian yawl, with a sail in mourning. What was our surprise, as we approached, when we discovered it to be the guide or carter on horseback with no less than five men clustering on to the poor beast.

It is customary for pedestrians to pay a halfpenny each for riding through the channel, and sometimes clinging before, sometimes hanging behind, or on one side, like rats on a cheese, the guide and his horse convey them over.

We were about to ask him to guide us across, but the load having dismouted, or tumbled off, when we were within a few yards of the brink, without a word he touched his hat, turned his horse round, and proceeded to retrace his course through the water. We followed. The crossing was wide but not deep ; and the sensation was that of swimming up the stream, so much so that for a moment we hesitated, when the quick eye of the guide immediately beckoned us forward. On the opposite bank we stopped, and the doffed hat exhibited a bronzed face, which had been exposed for many a long year to this hard life. The sixpence was thankfully received. " Good crossing to-day, Mr. Guide." " Yes, sur, never better ; but never so good that it is safe to stand still, sur, as you were doing." " How's that ?" " Why, not long since, on a fine bottom, a chaise was crossing, and the driver was drunk, and he did not stop more than three minutes, when the current washed the sand from under the wheels, and the chaise went over." " There is some danger, then, Mr. Guide " " Well, the drunken and heedless are always in danger, on sea or land." " What do you use the cart for, which stands on the bank ?" " When ladies or women as can't wade are crossing, I take them in it, you know, sur."

The guide, whose predecessors were maintained by the Priory of Conishead with the salary of three acres of land rent free, and fifteen marks per annum, now receives an annual stipend under patent of the Duchy of Lancaster,

King Henry VIII. having charged himself and his successors with the payment on the dissolution of the monasteries. He gave us a few directions, and we proceeded.

On reaching the shore we had the choice of pursuing our expedition in our own humble conveyance, or availing ourselves of the omnibus and railway, but, as we wished to understand Furness, we were not beguiled into the latter course. Our road led us through beautiful lanes, whose banks were spangled with flowers : the rich perfume of the honeysuckle scented the air, and the remains of the roses of summer showed what they must have been in their beauty. We admired the luxuriance of the corn-fields, which clothed every sloping hill-side, promising riches to the farmer. The golden harvest was interspersed with green crops, whose varied and delicate colour refreshed the eye, and contrasted well with the rich red soil of the fallow ground. We passed over rounded hills, which separate the basin-like valley, and paused to contemplate the primitive-looking secluded little villages hid in these hollows. Urswick, which was founded by the Britons, is perhaps unequalled by any in the kingdom for the peculiarly sheltered character of its situation. A lake-like piece of water embellishes the scene, in which the tidy farm-houses surrounding its margin are reflected ; the cattle were standing knee deep to cool themselves, ducks and geese complacently navigated the shallows, and an air of quiet serenity and self-containedness pervaded the place, as if the world of that valley was complete in itself. Dendron, too, with its old grey church tower, almost buried among sycamores, and its rural dwellings, attracted special attention.

The traveller is struck with the absence of trees in the

hedgerows throughout Furness, and we were told that this is one proof among many of the excellence of the system of farming adopted here. The lover of the picturesque must yield, but this circumstance gives a bareness to the general aspect of the country which the well known productiveness of its soil did not lead us to expect. There are other districts less attractive, but equally interesting, where mining operations are carried on, this being one of the leading sources of the wealth of Furness, and for which it was famous ere Saxon and Norman struggled for victory.

The ore is shipped at Barrow or Bardsea, for Carron and Swansea, where its superior quality finds purchasers, who use it to improve the poorer ores of Scotland and Wales. So rich is the metal, that the roads for miles are deeply dyed with the oxide of iron, and the houses, workmen, horses, pigs, and cattle,—(and, low be it said, the good dames also)—are all tinged with the same lurid colour. But we hasten towards Rampside, a little village at the extremity of the peninsula, and reach the last line of swelling hills between us and the sea. Upon the summit of this ridge stands the church,—its bare white walls and tower, whether or not built for the purpose, make it a most conspicuous landmark for miles, both seaward and landward.

Piel now lay before us. Its harbour was enlivened by vessels which had run in for safety, or to await a wind to waft them into Fleetwood or Liverpool. The masts are sometimes almost countless there. The island of Walney stretched away to the right, its long narrow form giving it much the appearance of an artificial breakwater. Beyond we saw the open sea,—and such a sea! True, as Wordsworth says, it may at times appear the " gentlest of all gentle things ;" but when, in stormy weather, the rolling surge beats upon the low shore of Walney, the noise of the waves, at the distance of many miles, resembles thunder. The apprehended danger of eruption from the sea was so great in the time of Queen Elizabeth, that the copyhold and customary tenants under the Crown, to whom " Wawney," as it was spelled after the dissolution of Furness Abbey, belonged, entered into covenant to keep the sea embankments in repair, and a special clause occurs which contemplates the possibility of the whole Island being submerged in the course of time. The embankments were first constructed by the monks of the Abbey, who repaired them with great care. From Rampside church we descend to the village, passing a few very prettily situated houses, in one of which the clergyman resides, where he conducts a respectable school in this healthy place.

The village consists of a line of houses close to the shore, which are by no means remarkable for their picturesque appearance, excepting one singular-looking old building, called Rampside Hall. It possesses a row of chimnies the whole length of the ridge of the roof, numerous enough to emit the " smokes" of all Rampside. They are commonly denominated the twelve apostles.

In the sixteenth century, behind the hall, there was a Rampside wood here. The herbage was let by special lease from the Crown in the time of Henry VIII., remarkable as the only lease for a term of years discovered by the commissioners of Parliament who examined into the property, "late the parcels and possessions of Charles Stewart," in Furness. A few stunted trees scarcely point out where the wood once grew.

The summer cottage of Wm. Gale, Esq., High Sheriff, is by far the most attractive residence. Its low elevation, consisting only of one story, is in good taste with the character of the objects around it. There is an inn in the village, and a shop, or rather *the* shop, where all the ordinary wants of man *and woman* may be supplied. It is well furnished with miscellaneous and multifarious articles, and though some fastidious people might think that the butter and bacon were in danger of coming in too close quarters with the ribbons and gown-pieces, and wonder why the calicoes were piled on the cheeses, the candles and herring hung on the sugar-barrel, and the soap claimed kindred with the pack of floor, doubtless the worthy mistress had her peculiar reasons for these odd juxtapositions in her own domain. Perhaps, as her size is of the magnificently comfortable or portly description, and her shop of the diminutively minute species, she finds it more convenient to have some of all sorts within arm's length.

Since the completion of the Furness Railway, Rampside has increased in importance, and, although of the numbers deposited here by the steamers, few care to stay in the journey, if further bound, many cross from Fleetwood for the day.

At the extremity of Rampside stands Concle Inn, which, though within a few yards of the village, is spoken of with the distinctiveness of a different territory. It must be that, in villages, the landlord of the inn being the chief personage, claims a sort of patronage over a peculiar province, and, as the Concle Inn is a new erection, it ranks as a sort of outside interloper, or squatter. We can answer, however, for the civility of the well-favoured dame under whose auspices it is kept.

From the Concle Inn an embankment is carried over the beach and sand for nearly a mile to Roe Island. Walking along it, on our way to the Castle, we crossed one of the wonders of Rampside, called Concle Hole,—a pool of salt water near the shore, which was formerly reputed to be unfathomable,—but there are few deeps, whether purses or abysses, which railway enterprize will not sound, and such has been the case here :—Huge piles have been firmly fixed in this " bottomless" vortex, and the spirit of credulity has vanished before the navvy and his incontrovertible demonstration.

Reaching Roe Island, we found modern improvements invading the sacred precincts of antiquity, but the broad girdle of a deep sea will, it is to be hoped, ever preserve the Isle of Fouldrey inviolate.

Roe Island was purchased a few years since by that man of marvellous enterprize, John Abel Smith, of whom it is said there is hardly a well-known country in the world to which his money has not been sent for works of enterprize or profit. Though only a few acres in extent, it now possesses a hotel, warehouse, custom-house, watch-tower, and many other facilities for carrying on an extensive trade, which is some day or other to be created.

From Roe to Piel Castle we had to use a boat, as Piel Harbour lies between the two points, and a beautifully broad and deep channel it is. Her Majesty's navy could shelter there, and, were the ships once in, they would lie as still as in a dock ; but a bar at the entrance, which cannot be crossed at low water, and which causes the security of the harbour, would, our companion feared, interpose impediments to their entrance. It has long been noted as a harbour, and when the monks made the district a centre of civilization, it had considerable exports and imports. At one period it was discovered that they thence regularly exported wool without paying duty, which was prohibited,—a rather striking evidence of the priests forgetting to render tribute to Cæsar. Did they ever forget to claim it for St. Peter or Mother Church?

Being ready to cross, we displayed a signal—and straightway we saw debouching from some rude comfortless looking cottages under the wall of the Castle, two boys and a girl, who hastened to launch a boat for us. They belong to a family residing near the inn, which is principally frequented by sailors when at anchor in the harbour, and which is noted for the special purity of the spirituous liquors sold there. Whiskey, Hollands, or real Jamaica, are all prime, it is said. French ships seldom touch there, so the brandy from that country may not be so much in request at Dick Hoole's.

The boat, with its crew of children, soon reached our side of the channel. They were a wild-looking set, but our doubts of their capacity for sailing were soon quieted by a by-stander, who assured us that these boys and girls, from babyhood, lived on the sea, and he had seen a girl sail a boat to a vessel to bring off a pilot, when no sailor durst venture. The sea ran mountain high, but the intrepid lass performed the feat with amazing dexterity and success. Ordinary storms are nothing to these daring little Chamleys, or to their father, whose predecessors have been pilots and fishermen, by profession, for generations. We certainly pitied them, and wished them nearer the superintendent care of some kind Christian, who might foster such energy in a still more useful direction, and a *less* exposed place. The day was calm, and the sea looked very green and very deep, and yet so clear that pebbles at the bottom were distinctly visible.

We had been so charmingly delayed on the road, that it was evening before we reached Fouldrey Island, and the shadows were falling far on the turf. We found the Castle towering above us,—"cased in the unfeeling armour of old time,"—with a calm and mournful dignity. Perhaps it might be owing to a lowering redness creeping over the heavens, or to the dense clouds darkening behind Black Combe, which imparted a stern and melancholy aspect to the massive walls of this ancient fortress; but we were told, and fully appreciate it, that, whether glowing in the gorgeous hues of a summer's sunset, or breasting the wild storms of a winter's sky, there hung over these time-worn battlements an impressive coldness and solemn character, which arrest the attention of every observer with a power peculiarly its own. There was no architectural ornament to attract, no striking historic facts to fix the mind upon any particular epoch in its existence; but, as we gazed, our thoughts reverted to the changing fortunes of our favoured land,—now the mistress of the seas and the arbiter of nations,—once the spoil and prey of contending bands of northern adventurers.

The Castle, whose ruins we beheld, was erected by an Abbot of Furness, in the reign of Edward III. But there are traces of a much earlier date to be discovered, which have led to the supposition that its foundations were laid by the Danes when they first ravaged our coasts in quest of plunder, and that this was one of their numerous places of refuge, whither they could retire when closely pressed by their enemies; and well is the situation fitted for such a purpose; separated from the main land by a deep channel, which would always afford safe shelter for their barques, protected by solid masonry and ditches, as strong on the land as on the sea side ;—these fierce sea-kings could devastate the rich vallies, and carry off the treasures of the inhabitants, which were more valuable than many of our readers may imagine,—and then retreating to Piel, could revel on the fruit of their foray, in the very sight of their victims.

Imagination pictures the consternation which the appearance of these pirate-fleets would occasion to the inhabitants, who, as successive bands of marauders landed on their coasts, saw themselves despoiled of their flocks and herds, their churches pillaged, and their lands wasted with fire and sword. The high prows of their Danish vessels were rendered doubly fearful by the terrific emblems they bore. They swept over the sea, to use their own poetic language, " in the tracks of the swans," whose migratory course they followed. The barques were navigated by men who laughed at the wind and waves. " The force of the storm," they sung, " is a help to the arm of the rower ; it carries us the way we would go." The wild war songs of these sons of Odin sounded over the waters—a fearful prelude to their work of devastation. They rushed to the combat without fear ; for their superstition taught them to believe that all who fell in battle were welcome to the Hall of Valhalla. The fragments of their highly figurative ballads which have been preserved give a terrible picture of the fierce fanaticism which animated them in their warfare,—a fearful warfare for this country, only just recovering from the prolonged contest which had ended in the confirmation of the Saxon rule.

But we must refrain from dwelling on the dark scenes of that stirring period, when the Saxon, lately an invader himself, quailed before the raven banner, unfurled by another tribe of his own family,—and when the light of Christianity, just kindled, was a second time threatened with extinction by the dark mythology of Scandinavia. The time was not long before the Norman subjected both, and the Anglo-Saxon and the Anglo-Dane groaned together beneath the iron yoke of the conqueror.

Then the new lords of the soil partitioned the conquered territory among their followers, and most of the rich district of Furness, including the island upon which Piel Castle stands, soon became the property of the Church. Stephen, Count of Blois, afterwards King of England, devoted that portion of his possession to the foundation of a religious house in the year 1127. And after two centuries, when the Norman monks had erected their beautiful Abbey, and when their wealth and power had so much increased that their abbots united with their priestly character the authority of princes, they erected a strong fortress at Piel, upon the old Danish foundations, to defend their territory from aggression and to protect their commerce.

We can form but little idea now of the original extent of the Piel of Fouldrey. The waves, which have submerged a great portion of the outworks, now wash the walls of the castle itself. Sufficient remains to prove the vast extent of the fortifications; but the time will probably come, when the stealthy but irresistible power of the sea will destroy this relic of that by-gone age, when feudal rights and privileges were paramount in the land. The double line of walls and the two series of ditches and bridges are still traceable in the green sward, showing what a sturdy defence the garrison could make under attack.

We have dwelt too long, perhaps, on these matters, and yet the more we can multiply our associations with the memorials of the habits and pursuits of the men of former times, the more interest shall we feel in visiting the remains of those edifices which attest, by their strength or their magnificence, the importance which was attached to the two grand rivals for power of that day—the sword and the church.

The massive and lasting character of this erection, whose earliest walls were built of the round stones gathered from the beach, and cemented with a mass of mortar or compost, is proved by a huge block of the fortification, which consists altogether of this conglomerate, having laid for twenty years in the sea,—thrown down by its undermining powers—and yet there is no decay of the lime which binds the rubble together, and it is almost impossible to remove one of these boulders from its adopted matrix. As the tide arose we took a boat, that we might attain a view of the Castle from the sea. Passing outwards, our boatman described the extent of the fortifications, which are still occasionally apparent under water, and are met with about half a mile from the present ruins; but whether these be old Danish remains, or the more modern monkish, we could not decide. We had a strange feeling when sailing above these ruined walls, which once reverberated with noisy revels, or the groans of the prisoner. Father Time had been busy here, and this rude strong-hold—with a portion of its bulwarks buried deep in the sea—was a testimony to the character of all earthly things!

We returned homeward under the darkened shade of the old Castle, through whose windows the grey light of a wild moonlight sky was gleaming. We landed on the railway embankment, found comfortable refeshment at the Concle Hotel, and dreamt of Vikings, armed Monks, railway works, and locomotives, and the wonderful succession of events in the record of old England's history.

CHAPTER VIII.

DALTON.—FURNESS ABBEY.—ALDINGHAM.—BARDSEA, AND ULVERSTON.

FURNESS ABBEY

CHAPTER VIII.

WE reserved a visit to Furness Abbey for our return from Piel Castle, intending to vary the route, in order that we might embrace some of the many places of interest which are found in this district. We first proceeded to Dalton, leaving the ruins on our right hand; but so completely concealed in a deep glen or "gill," that we should have had no idea of their proximity had not some time-worn massy grey walls attracted our attention, showing that the boundaries of the Abbey grounds had at one time far exceeded their present limits.

Dalton was the manorial court and market town of the monks of Furness Abbey. Its prominent situation and its vicinity to the iron mines had caused the Romans to establish a camp there, and the remains of their fortifications are still to be found. A Castle succeeded when the Abbots acquired possession. The situation was admirably adapted for the purpose, as it was sufficiently near to keep up constant intercourse with the monks at the Abbey, whilst the noise and turmoil of the extensive civil affairs which their wide jurisdiction involved, did not intrude upon the solemn seclusion of their own beautiful vale.

The Castle was situated on the escarpment of a considerable hill, and such were its natural defences that it required very few from art. The remains of the feudal system are still exhibited in the courts baron, which are held twice a year in the square tower which formed part of the ancient Castle, and appears to have been erected in the reign of Edward III. The situation commands a plentiful and unfailing supply of water, which must have greatly enhanced its value as a place of defence.

The present town is not very attractive, although there are a few neat comfortable-looking dwellings. It consists of one long street, and, when we had satisfied our curiosity, we branched off by an abrupt angular turn to the Abbey. By this road we had approached these beautiful ruins on a former visit, and, without wishing to draw invidious comparisons between the past and the present railway era, it is with our first impressions that we present the reader.

We entered by the northern gateway, along a shaded lane, with a rich meadow to our left, inclosed by a steep wooded bank. Before us was the rich dark foliage of the lofty trees in which the Abbey is embosomed, producing the effect of a massive frame to a beautiful picture. The verdant green sward in the foreground, as we passed through the portals of the manor-house, was a charming relief to the mellow tinting of the time-stained walls and the luxuriantly-clustering ivy which mantles around them.

The effect produced upon us was truly impressive. The railway had not then broken the solitude of ages. Silence reigned throughout the Valley of Nightshade, and our voices were hushed to a whisper, in sympathy with the solemnity of the scene. We stood in the centre of the roofless nave of the building, and marked the fragments of beautifully sculptured ornaments which lay around us, half hidden among the long-tangled grass and ferns, and encrusted with moss and lichen. There were the broken shafts of the gigantic columns which had once supported the lofty roof ; and, looking to the west, the tall slender pillars of the ruined tower, with its festoons of ivy, gave us some idea of the majestic sublimity which had inspired the erection of this venerable structure.

But the east presents the greatest variety of objects, and admiration soon absorbed every other feeling, when we examined the remains of this beautiful edifice in that direction.

To those who have never seen what we might vainly endeavour to describe, words would feebly and incorrectly delineate the scene; but it is impossible to visit that fascinating locality without bringing away some mental picture of beauty, in which some individual object stands forth in prominent relief, and to which memory loves to turn with never-fading interest. About the locutorium, the scriptorium, the refectory, the dormitory, the kitchens, &c., we cared but little, for whatever may be said as to the care of the monks for their own comforts in these respects, we must confess that we entertain no very exalted idea of the *domestic arrangements* of a race of beings who excluded from their prescriptive rights the better half of civilized life; we, therefore only felt interested in these divisions of the building so far as they contributed to the picturesque effect of the whole.

But it was impossible to refuse our unqualified tribute of admiration to the highly-ornamented choir and chapter-house ; and we formed some conception of that beautiful arrangement of architectural skill which so designed the latter as to impart to it the brightest light and the deepest shade. There was the reflected glow of the evening sun streaming through the broken windows, and casting its golden hues upon the sculptured fragments of stone, while the shadows of the uncertain light, beyond its influence, were deepened into the gloom of twilight.

Attractive as this erection was, it is on one beautiful arch of magnificent proportions that we love to think. Its graceful line is still perfect,—the light and aspiring shafts which sustain its chaste form are garlanded with an airy and elegant fringe of wild flowers, which cling to the decaying stones as if anxious to add yet another charm to its perfect symmetry. No nightshade clustered from its clefts,—no gloom hung upon its aged but beautiful brow. The gorgeous glows of eventide gleamed through it, and imparted tints of unearthly glory to the lofty structure ; and we thought of the days when the white-robed monks, —rejoicing in their Easter festivals with songs of exultation, and with the perfume of Eastern incense floating around them,—paced along these now deserted aisles.

In favoured spots, like Bekangs Gill, or the " Valley of Nightshade," they reared their stately edifices on a scale of magnificence and splendour which shames the unsubstantial erections of modern days. They consecrated their richest and their best to the work. The solid masonry of the walls tells us that they wrought not for their own generation merely, but that the *enduring* church was the idea in their minds. The *glory* of that church they sought to embody in the exquisite beauty of the architectural ornaments and the richness of the internal decorations. They enlisted in their service the skill of the most accomplished artists, they imposed upon their employees no fettering estimates of expense, but bid them upraise a sanctuary, meet for the worship of the Lord of Heaven and of Earth.

In that sanctuary learning and art were encouraged and grew, and to its embellishment and glorification much of both were exclusively devoted. The idea of eternity, stability, and beauty, which had at first been realised in dwelling upon the excellency of a pure devotion, became centred in the forms and accompaniments of the worship, instead of the spiritual worship itself. Thus much of the zeal which was expended in the foundation of the means to a great end,—namely, the propagation of truth—only secured an apparatus which absorbed the energies of the future devotees. The times must, however, always form the medium of judgment; and when we remember the darkness which overshadowed christendom, we need not wonder that some gloom and mist dimmed the sanctuary.

In Furness there is no doubt that the influence of the monks was useful, and that a cultivation and civilization followed their establishment which would not otherwise have been attained. They do not appear to have liberated their theowes or bondmen, as many religious houses and religious men did, but they protected and encouraged them, and, under their guardianship, Furness became the garden of Lancashire.

With far different feelings do we contemplate the Castle of the Warrior! To reach the dismantled fortress of the once ferocious and powerful baron, we have to scale a lofty hill, and with the massive keep and hollowed dungeons we recall the feudal tyranny which exacted the most debasing services, and offered no particle of instruction in return.

The barren rock, on which his stronghold stands, bespeaks robbery and devastation, and then the safe keeping of his plunder. But to the lowly valley and sequestered glen we must turn our footsteps when we would find the crumbling dwelling of the monk. Let taste go with us, for the loveliness of the site must be a key to its discovery. Moreover, the well-cultivated region will indicate the energy which improved, as well as the skill which neglected not, the advantages to be derived from the vicinity of pellucid streams and fertile lands.

The locomotive engine announces to us that the days of monasticism are over. We can only hope that such energy as the human mind spent in Bekangs Gill may never be devoted to a more injurious end, and the sternest condemner of asceticism, when he reprobates the erection of such buildings as Furness Abbey, must confess that these remains of ecclesiastical architecture impart an additional charm to the quiet and picturesque scenery amidst which they are generally found ; while the sage and the moralist can point to the crumbling ruin as the truth-telling monument of the instability and evanescent nature of the noblest and best of man's handiworks. And let the disciple of progress, who sees only in the wonderful developement of man's intellectual energy, a theme for self-glorification, learn a lesson from the scene before him. As he rushes through this peaceful valley on the wings of steam, let him ask himself whether, while he justly rejoices in the possession of a more enlightened religious faith, which has unchained his mind and emancipated his reason, he is using all his multiplied advantages with as single an aim to the glory of God, as did the monks of Furness.

Thoughts such as these occupied our minds as we quitted the Abbey and pursued a cross-road which led us through shady lanes till within view of the shore. Below us was the tower of Aldingham Church, in a most picturesque situation; while the bay, with its distant and charming variety of scenery, formed the back-ground.

This church is surrounded by a small grave-yard, which abuts on to the beach. Both seem as if they were supernumerary, except as adjuncts to the scene; for no village, no public-house, no rows of cottages or scattered dwellings are visible. One deserted mansion stands opposite to it, and the servants at the substantial stables of the Rectory, which hides itself in some lovely garden-ground behind the church, are the only evidences that there may possibly be living worshippers for that ancient temple. Such is the conformation of Furness, that, in the deep hollows of the billowy earth,—(for the whole of the peninsula assumes that form, or rather, as an acquaintance once observed, it looks as if daguerreotyped into present shape when in the process of bubbling up from the action of internal fire,)—there are hidden nooks and corners where the substantial farmer and the industrious peasant live in peace and prosperity. To a passing visitor Furness would appear deserted; but a Sunday at Aldingham (and it would not be lost time) brings forth a spontaneous harvest of churchgoers, numerous enough to astonish the stranger, and make him inquire whence they all came. The venerable incumbent* is worthy of the edifice. Age and learning seem to belong to a place whose attractiveness, like an illumi-

* Dr. STONARD is since removed to another world, and succeeded by the Rev. J. MACAULEY, the brother of the eminent statesman and historian.

nated manuscript, bids the wayfaring man enquire into the hidden and ancient treasures of Aldingham.

These hasty sketches must not, however, lose themselves in the dense mistiness of past ages ; otherwise we would stop to ascertain something about the sites and acreage of the ancient places Rhos, Lies, and Crimelton, which the sea has washed away, and whose sole relics are the musty parchments which gave them to Furness Abbey. Neither can we delay our journey to measure the extent of the once-populous town of Aldingham, its castle and its defences, which imparted pride and dignity to its Saxon Thane, and bestowed a title on the Lord de Harrington, who died at the head of the troops of Furness, fighting under the Red Rose at the bloody battle of Wakefield.

The place of this populous city now knows it no more, and, like those of Phœnicia and Philistia, the fisherman spreads his net, and the barge and the sloop sail where Aldingham flourished in the days of its prosperity.

But we must take a walk to the terraced mound, standing about a mile from the church, which distance is supposed to indicate the extent of the town. The moat is crossed by a substantial bank where the bridge once stood, and a regularly sloping approach on the northern side enables the visitor to reach the summit without climbing the terraces. The sea, that great enemy to antiquarians,—himself the greatest piece of antiquity,—is gnawing away the south-east side, and will, it is to be feared, ere long, remove this ancient mound. Standing upon its summit, the modern historian can connect the progressive epochs of English chronology, and feel that he occupies a place which Briton, Roman, Saxon, and Norman have successively trod. But to the pages of other works we must refer the antiquarian student, only assuring him that Aldingham is still a field but half explored, and that much remains for him to discover and interpret.

From Aldingham we pursued a beautiful foliage-curtained lane to Baycliffe, which is a village whose surrounding scenery is more interesting than itself, and yet there is a quiet sobriety about the place which becomes its mature age. The name is easily explained, and the bay running in at the foot of the cliff translates the term.

Prosecuting our journey, we soon entered Sea-wood, a most romantic extent of coppice plantation. It appears to cover some hundreds of acres, and its winding pathways, discovering curious rocks washed into deep crevices by the percolation of water, or standing up in all manners of form, with here and there a mountain ash crowning the hoary natural pillar, and flourishing on its pinnacle many feet from the ground, while wild flowers in abundance gem the sod, form a most delicious shelter in the mid-day heat, or the quiet repose of eventide.

At the entrance is the old manor-house, where the courts of the Duchy of Lancaster are still held. We could not ascertain whether this property was a reservation made by King John, when, as Duke palatine, in his necessities, he sold the neighbouring manor, or whether it was annexed to the Duchy, and so became the appanage of the present infant prince, at the time when Furness and Conishead were despoiled of their revenues by Henry the Eighth.

About half way through the wood a delicious prospect burst upon us,—the whole of the Ulverston bay, with Bardsea, Conishead, and the distant mountains coming into view. Through the wood, we again reached the beach, and the steamer at the pier, and the multifarious vehicles for conveying away its passengers, the unprepossessing " bus," the inelegant tub car, and the much more picturesque donkey shandry-cart, gave to Bardsea a life and busy look which, we understand, are now gone for ever.

Bardsea is a very attractive place, and, were it near a crowded population, would soon lose the rusticity which is its peculiar charm. Its few little cottages strewed hither and thither are, " in the season," crammed full of maids and children, who delight in the shady lanes and the tidal beach ; and the walks past the Well House, the antique and picturesque residence of the late Thomas Petty, Esq., or up to the green where the school is taught, and where episcopal service was considerately provided by the neighbouring clergymen on Sunday afternoons, before the erection of the church, are full of subjects of interest and admiration to the botanist and the artist. The new church wants age to lend a shading pencil to its glaring limestone before it will add beauty to the scene, but the erection of such a commodious and substantial structure, by liberal donations and munificent voluntary subscriptions, elicits the benevolent sympathies of the lover of the picturesque, and disarms all criticism.

Bardsea Hall adjoins the village. There we can invite our readers without any apology. We wish we could sketch it for them. Erected by the Molyneux family, it is now going to decay for the want of an occupant, although the neighbourhood, for climate and scenery, makes it a most tempting situation. It has been a matter of dispute whether this or Well House was the site of the Hospital of St. John of Jerusalem, which formerly existed at Bardsea, and must have been one of the first of the class, as it was in being in the latter part of the eleventh century, and within a very few years of the institution of the parent establishment at Jerusalem, the foundation of the extensive and powerful order of Knights Hospitallers. We are inclined to believe that Bardsea Hall is the more probable locality, if the hospital really stood at Bardsea, and not elsewhere; for, after the establishment of Conishead as a priory, William, son of Roger de Berdesey, gave to it a quantity of land in Berdesey, together " with a croft in which the house of the hospital of Jerusalem stood."

Conishead Priory, whose park is entered after leaving Bardsea, offers numerous inducements to tempt the visitor to delay. The remembrance of the old Conventual Edifice is entirely lost in the splendid mansion which is reared upon its foundations. Nothing beyond the loveliness of the country and the ruin on Chapel Island indicates the taste and skill of the canons of St. Augustine. We regret this, for howsoever beautiful the architectural works of modern times,—howsoever grand or ornamental may be the structures of a Pugin or a Wyatville,—we find a solid magnificence in the ancient exercise of the art, which the towers and turrets of the present Conishead do not realize.

But we will not quarrel with the English-gothic now so much in fashion, for he must have been a most unskilful hand who could have made any other than a picturesque building in a place so full of native beauty,—and to the traveller in search of variety, the Priory, as it is, has a multitude of charms. The rooms are on a noble scale, with an entrance hall which has been contrived to preserve some of the relics of the conventual church, and is of dimensions adequate to the conception of a princely dwelling. The cloisters are ornamental, and retain the character of the old in the new edifice. The conservatories and flower-gardens are worthy of this most favourable climate, and we concluded that he who shall be the future purchaser of this abode, if gifted with means adequate to its tasteful completion and liberal occupation—if endowed with a mind in unison with a country so profuse in nature's noble gifts—and if blessed with a heart generous to his neighbours and thankful to his God—will be the possessor of the ingredients which constitute happiness below.

Conishead traces its name to an ancient tongue. It was originally written Coningheved, which is supposed to indicate the place where a British king had been buried, and being afterwards used as a boundary mark by the Saxons, was called the Cyning, or Conyings, or King's Head. A similar appropriation of the term occurs in Conistone, where a stone, erected over the grave of a British chief, or a place where he administered judgment, is called Cyning, or Conyngstone, now Conistone. The neighbouring village claims a name of a British origin, and Bertesig, or "a place of thickets or coppice," as written in the Doomsday survey, was softened by Norman tongue to Berdesey. Aldingham, whatever may have been its British name, said to be "Altig," a place of cliffs, which, when compounded with "ham," a habitation, in Saxon,—made up the Aldingham of the present day—had become a bona fide and unmistakeable Saxon word, and conveyed to that people the idea of "ancient town, or town where the law was administered."

From Conishead we proceeded towards Ulverstone, but being attracted by a union jack, mounted with considerable display on a little homely thatched cottage amongst a cluster of houses, we were informed that this hamlet, with the unaristocratic name of Dragley Beck, was the birth-place of the late most estimable secretary to the Admiralty, Sir John Barrow, and this humble one-storied cot was his paternal residence. It was most gratifying to observe that the praiseworthy qualities which had won high distinction and most important place, were not forgetful of the lowly position whence their possessor had sprung, but year by year had recognised it by this public exhibition, as well as by extensive charitable distributions on each return of his natal day.

Ulverstone is a place of considerable trade, and with a better approach to the sea, would absorb the bulk of the imports and exports of the district, but so long as the canal is only accessible at very high tides, it must retain its character of a second-rate port ; more especially since vessels laden with goods for Ulverstone will be able shortly to avoid all the difficulties of the navigation from Piel to Bardsea, by discharging their cargoes at Barrow, and forwarding them by railway to Ulverstone. This railway is now in course of construction. We were informed that several engineers have advised the diversion of the waters of the Crake and the Leven into the canal, so as effectu-ally to scour out at all tides a ship course from Ulverstone to the sea, and that land could be thereby enclosed which would more than compensate for the cost of the work. It may be so, but we must leave the question in the hands of the engineers (who are not always true pro-phets) and the Ulverstone people, who seem well able to look after their own interests, for what with advertise-ments and hand-bills, steam-boats and steam-engines, coaches, cars, and yachts, they appear determined to make their pretty little town the key to the Lakes and to Cumberland. The vigour and untiring energy they display on this head is most admirable. They throw out their tempting lines of steam transit in all directions from Piel, reminding us of the industrious insect which projects its films from bough to bough, and weaves a mesh of unavoidable extent and density : only the good people of Furness usher you, when captive, to good accommodation, slow travelling, and most delightful scenery.

From Ulverstone, by Atkinson's far-famed coach, noted for the civility of the driver, we proceed to Newby Bridge. The road skirts the high ground produced by the extensions of the Conistone ranges of hills to the sea, and opens out sweet prospects up the valleys, which run towards the higher mountains. The Leven flows at our right hand till we reach Backbarrow, where Mr. Ainsworth's tasteful cotton mills extract, from this picturesque river, the sinewy power for turning the spinning machinery, which is won in Lancashire from the muscular beam of the steam-engine.

Here also are some of the antique forges for making Backbarrow iron, peculiar from being worked with charcoal. Time out of mind was this process carried on far away amongst the hills, on the rushing streamlet of Cunsey and Grisedale Beck, until the reign of Elizabeth, when the bloomeries were discontinued, on account of the spoliation they occasioned to her Majesty's woods in those parts,—being portions of the royal spoil of Furness Abbey,—and the rent which they paid, twenty pounds per annum, was assessed under the name of bloomsmithy-rate, upon all the neighbouring herdwicks or farms.

Backbarrow is as pleasing as a manufacturing village can well be.

Thence to Newby Bridge we followed the left bank of the rolling Leven river, noted for its excellent fisheries, attributable to its waters flowing out of Windermere.

At Newby Bridge we reached the outskirts of the lake district. There is a retired comfortable Hotel, where Mr. White was exceedingly civil, and a walk to a summer-house behind his garden, on a lofty hill, gave us a delight-ful view of the neighbourhood.

The object which most attracted our attention was a long wooded mountain range, extending for miles up the east side of Windermere, and called, we were told, Cart-mel Fells. As the proximity of Cartmel to Grange sounded like home, we were tempted to make some en-quiries, and found that Cartmel Fells was an extensive and romantic district of high rocky land (Teutonic "felz") with cultivated hollows and wooded glens.

We resolved to explore them; and, early next morn-ing, rambled among this hilly region, which comprehends some most magnificent prospects. At last we reached a solitary house by the side of a road, which descends pre-cipitously into the inclosed and winding valley of Wither-slack.

There was an aspect of quietness about it and its build-ings which attracted our attention. A variety of convey-ances near it roused our curiosity; and we were told, on reaching it, that it was a quakers' meeting-house, called " Height," and the place of worship usually frequented by those members of that society who frequent Grange. The name is most appropriate. There it stood on the lofty head of a mighty brow, at the very verge of the unenclosed mountains ; looking down into the distant vallies, like a contemplative spirit surveying the world below. A grave yard, with a few mounds of earth—no more—was near it. It stood higher than the place of worship ; not a stone told the name of the dead—we were left to conjecture even the age by the size of the upheaved grassy sod. The sun was shining joyously, and the grasshopper was singing his monotonous song. A humble bee passed by, but his busy tones seemed lost in that wide waste, and, till he hung upon some white clover, we wondered what sweets he could find there ; as it was, he seemed far above his ordinary track. A grey plover shot above us with his shrill whistle, and some lapwings fluttered incessantly around, as if they discovered us to be aliens. A cloud for a moment dimmed the sun, and we thought how cold that graveyard would be, and we did not wish to be laid there.

A very small cottage was discovered, adjoining the meeting-house, inhabited by some humble but " honest-spoken friends ;" and understanding there was a " meeting for worship" going to be held on the occasion of a " public friend" being there, we resolved to attend it.

A small covered porch in a high wall brought us into a court, which must afford some shelter in this bleak place to the meeting-house. Through another porch, with seats at its sides, on which were seated some female quakers while the men were attending to the fastening up of their horses (for they all appeared to come from a distance), we entered into this modest house of prayer. Though loftier, it was not much larger than a good-sized room. The seats were of unpainted wood, being ordinary forms, placed in rows on each side the apartment—the male friends at one side, and the females at the other. At the top of the room there was a long raised seat, in which sat three friends, two men and a woman. Behind us was an apartment, raised over the adjoining cottage, entered by some steps from the meeting-house, which we were told by a communicative young female, was the women's meeting, where they conducted "their discipline," which we understood to be a sort of investigation by the ancient order of deaconesses, now in disuetude in other churches, into the conduct and demeanour of the female part of their community. On entering, there was no bowing or taking off the hat; each sat down, and immediately assumed the appearance of perfect stillness. We noticed one pale-faced venerable-looking *young* man, and we doubt whether he moved a muscle once during the whole time, excepting on the occasion of a prayer being offered up, when he arose, stood erect as a pillar, covering his face with his hat, and, at its conclusion, subsided into the same death-like quiet.

There were seventeen friends present, eleven women and six men. At first we looked around us, but soon the touching stillness of our neighbours crept over us. The sympathies of the place entered our hearts. We were in a solitary temple, which, from a date on a stone outside, appeared to have been erected soon after George Fox began "his ministry," when there must have been still less cultivation near it than there is now. The situation was probably chosen to elude those arbitrary officers of power, who haled out the men and women of this peaceable community, and cast them, not by tens or scores, but by hundreds, into loathsome dungeons. There was not a human sound to be heard,—no people were astir amongst those lonely heights of the ancient hills. A few stunted trees grew in the court-yard; the breeze stirred their leaves, and a small redbreast chaunted its solitary notes in their boughs. His thread-like tones proved that other sounds were not there to mingle with them.

The house within was apparently a living grave,—silence reigned supreme! But there were deep internal feelings, and the moistened eye in some ; and the suppressed but perceptible heaving of the struggling soul in others, spoke of spiritual thoughtfulness and awful feeling.

The air was cool, almost chilly, for dampness hung on the little-used walls. The wood of the floor was green, and we felt a cold thrill through our whole frame; but powerful is the sympathy of soul with soul, and the deep introversion of those silent worshippers grew upon us, and in the utter motionless and absence of quivering sound, our hearts became oppressed with a sense of the littleness of man and the mightiness of the Divinity. Then, on the raised seat alluded to, there knelt down the " public friend," who proved to be a woman preacher, " travelling through Lancashire, with a certificate from her own meeting that she was a minister in good esteem at home." All rose up and stood while this female, in a clear voice of musical sweetness, but uttered with a tone of the deepest abasement, prayed to the most High for the outpouring of the spirit upon all flesh. As she proceeded her fervor increased and rose to a pitch of intense earnestness, almost assuming the modulated intonation of a chaunt ; again and again she suddenly resumed her whispering accents, until again and again her fervor seemed to ring through the little temple, and then she suddenly ceased, and the seats were resumed. The prayer of the preacher had carried every heart with it, and stifled sobs and the loud-heaving of the choking sigh were distinctly heard for a moment, and all was still. No preaching or other religious ceremony followed, but, after half an hour's continued solemn silence, the friends in the raised seat shook hands, next those below, my neighbour offered her hand to me, which being accepted, mine was heartily shaken, and the meeting broke up.

We found that the " members" staid to " transact their discipline," as it was " monthly meeting day," and that the men and women sit apart. Our communicative friend accompanied us a short way homeward, and told us that George Fox's wife, the widow of Judge Fell, of Ulverstone, used to attend Height Meeting frequently, and conducted the discipline. She informed us something about the friends " dealing," that is, giving advice, in George Fox's days, to a humble widow who sold lace and ribbons to her neighbours, and who was reproved for encouraging "the world's ways and finery," and as we looked upon our companion's cheerful face, encircled with the finest muslin, and the smart gold chain, with the neat little gold watch at her girdle, &c., &c., we mused how Mrs. Fox would have " dealt" with her.

But George Fox was a wonderful man. While all the countless competing sects of the Commonwealth days, excepting the large masses of Baptists and Independents, have disappeared, the followers of this stern and uncompromising reformer, ever feeble in numbers, but always powerful in principle, stand as memorials of adhesion one to another, in an unflinching negation of a "hireling ministry." We were told that this little meeting house was used summer and winter. Bleak must be the road to it, and inhospitable the welcome on those dreary heights

K

in winter's coldest days. A very few of the Society live in the neighbourhood, and often only two or three meet and hold their silent worship : sometimes only one, and scarcely ever more than ten or twelve, excepting when quaker visitors to Grange are numerous. Such was the information we received.

The road from Height to Grange was full of objects of interest, but our thoughts could not banish the impressions received in the solemn stillness of that mountain house of prayer.

Conclusion.

St. Paul's Church, Grange-over-Sands.

CONCLUSION.

AFTER rambling over the neighbourhood, we always arrived at Grange with the feeling of a homely return. We were much impressed with the unostentatious character of the inhabitants, the proper relations of rank in the little community being admirably maintained. When the richer aid with kind civility their poorer neighbours, and the poorer return with respectful independence the courtesy of the more affluent, it gives a healthy tone to the mental atmosphere, and such appears to be the simple and satisfactory condition of things at Grange, for it is one of those communes where mutual dependance and good-heartedness are freely and fully practised. You may go far through England to find a village in which the social bond of neighbourhood is in so healthful a state, and in no country in the world, except our own, can be found that happy medium between the servility of eastern manners and the abrupt rudeness of American republicanism—called civilization.

We have no sympathy with cringing subserviency, but we do like to see the laws of good-breeding pervading a state, and we have seen as true a gentleman in mind and bearing in the humble attire of a yeoman or peasant as can be found in the drawing-rooms of Belgravia.

There is something in the charm of natural politeness which we would define to be the expression of the kindly feelings of a truly benevolent heart, which is irresistibly winning in whatever rank of life it is met with ; and we are bound to say, that, not only at Grange, but in our rambles through Furness, we have been much gratified with observing the prevalence of this becoming ornament.

One advantage which Grange possesses is its proximity to the Lake District. We reach Windermere after a pleasant ride of a few miles—seven we believe, but must not be positive, for no two persons agree as to the *exact* distance, and most differed as to the best route. At last we discovered that the judgment was governed by the topographical situation of the adviser, and that those who lived at the north end of the village recommend the Lindale direction, and those at the south end the Cartmel route ; with either the visitor will be pleased, but, if he travel on foot or on horseback, we would counsel him to search out a blind sort of lane situated between the two, as the most delightful, if not the nearest.

To Windermere we often bent our steps, and thither we advise others to go also. We do not profess, with the ladies of the lake country, to throw the filmy line and wield the bending rod, and sport with the foolish fancy of the poor fish for the delusive but barbed fly (alas, how often imitated in human kind!) We cannot, therefore, pronounce beyond hearsay upon the advantages of Windermere for the exercise of the piscatorial art. But if disqualified to judge of the fishing, we can at least testify to the delight which many other enjoyments, peculiar to the district, are calculated to afford. We could expatiate upon the pleasures of sailing, rowing, botanizing, rambling in the woods, scrambling up the rocks, and climbing the fortress heights of the mighty mountain bulwarks of Westmorland and Cumberland; but Grange is too far from these regions to include them in a description of its legitimate domains; indeed they claim the exercise of a more qualified pen.

We must now conclude these slight sketches of this interesting locality : there still remain unnoticed many a charming wooded nook and quiet glen, where weakly and delicate invalids may find the repose so grateful to them ; and we have shown that, for the more enterprising visitor, there is abundant scope for the exercise of his more vigorous powers.

A few weeks had flown rapidly by in the enjoyment of the scenes described in the foregoing pages, when a summons from our southern home obliged us to break up the associations and pleasures which had so delightfully filled up the time of our stay, and given us a sort of citizenship feeling in this little community.

We quitted Grange with our feelings of affection still clinging to its picturesque scenery ; and while endeavouring to describe, though very imperfectly, a few of the most striking features of this attractive locality, our memory has been refreshed and gladdened by recalling the simple pleasures we enjoyed there.

It is true that the hand of time shatters our pleasant pictures, and in no new combination of circumstances do we ever revive the same emotions of delight. The touch of sorrow too often changes this beautiful world into a vale of tears ; but happy are they who, with a heart alive to the bounties of God in creation, have been enabled, by His grace, to regard them as foretastes of a brighter and happier world.

JOHN HUDSON, PRINTER, KENDAL.

LIST OF SUBSCRIBERS

The publisher thanks the following people who
subscribed to the book's publication

Stewart E. Allen, Cartmel

Joe Alston, Lancaster

John & Mary Andrew, Kent's Bank

Tom Andrews, Kent's Bank

Eileen Arthur, Kendal

Dr M W Arthurton, Cartmel

Mr & Mrs J A Ashworth, Kent's Bank Road

Mrs Nancey C Atkinson, Morecambe Bank

Alan Boyes, Priory Lane

David G Bentham, Priory Lane

Mrs Margaret Baker, Methven Road

Peter Birtwistle, Allithwaite

Robert Box, Allithwaite

William Bateman, Flookburgh

Amos Burton, Grange Fell Road

David Gordon Borrowdale, Methven Road

May & Vernon Bryan, Kent's Bank

Mr & Mrs L O Braysher, Grange

Mrs Hetty Bond, Mississauga, Ontario

M F T Barrett, Rainhill

Eric H H Barker, Grange Fell Road

Sandra Barton, Priory Lane

AE Bird, Grange Fell Road

Eve Bernstein, Main Street

Mr & Mrs M Beresford, Flookburgh

Keith & Vivien Benton, Kirkhead Road

M S Bramley, Barber Green

J H Bramley, Barcelona

Ken Bird, Cark

Jim Banks, Cark

Rev A D Briddock, Kent's Bank

Jack W Berrett, Marlow Bottom

Barrow Public Library

James Bell, Ulverston

Mrs Sylvia Brown, Kentsford Road

Oliver & Emily Bowsher, Methven Road

Roman Cizdyn, Lancaster

Gordon Christie, Barrow

Ken Cholerton, Great Head

James Christopherson, Flookburgh

J E Chorley, Cartmel

Mollie C Points, Eden Mount

Miss P Clay, Lindale

Rachel Coaton, Stockport

Mrs Mary Crayston, Rockland Road

Mike Crowe, Dearden Close

Mr & Mrs E Croft, Main Street

Veronica Cameron, Cart Lane

Charles Crosbie, Allithwaite Road

Dorothy Crosbie, Allithwaite Road

Dorothy M Clark, Melling

Dr Jean Carroll, Kentsford Road

Terry Carter, Allithwaite

Geoff Chadwick, Wyke, W Yorkshire

Julian & Barbara Davies, Flookburgh

Mr & Mrs F W Durigan, Berners Close

Steven Duncan, High Newton

Howard W Elliott, Milnthorpe

Ronald Errington, Flookburgh

Mrs Brenda Eakhurst, Allithwaite

Margaret & David Eastlick, Highfield Road

Daniel Elsworth, Ulverston

Robert & Margaret Egan, Allithwaite

Liz Fell, Allithwaite

Alan & Jennifer Forsyth, Cartmel Fell

Andrew Fairey & Bruno Guillon, Cart Lane

Wilfred Fishwick, The Orchard

Louise Freeman, Tadworth

John Garbutt, Allithwaite

Mr & Mrs A R Grundy, Charney Road

F Kevin Gibson, Prestwich

Grange-Over-Sands Library

David A Gee, Allithwaite

David & Penny Gray, formerly of Milton Terrace

Mrs M Carole Gregory, Risedale

Mary & Colin Guest, The Old Nurseries

Alec Hornby, Flookburgh

David Lincoln Hodgson, Kilmidike Drive

Mr J & Mrs B Habron, Berry Bank Road

Derek William Hughes, Highfield Road

William J Harrison, Castle Cary

Mr & Mrs E G Higgins, Cartmel

Stuart W Harling, Rotary Club

Mrs Margaret Hobson, Meadow Grove

Dr. M P & Mrs S M Houghton, Charney Road

Mrs Angela Sheila Herbert, Lindale

Mr & Mrs M A Hancox, Staveley-in-Cartmel

K M Hutton, Fellside Court

Teresa Howes, Lancaster

Jean Hawksley, Hampsfell Road

Jean Hunnam, Priory Crescent

Helen & Mike Hill, Linden Fold

Pat Howarth, Pillaton, Cornwall

Barrie Hilton, Station Square

Roy Hilton, Wymeswold

Mrs Ann Hodgson, nee Burrow, Allithwaite

Edwin & Alison Howarth, Lytham St. Annes

Gary M Holden, Flookburgh

Maggie Helliwell, Main Street

Geoffrey Holme, Barrow in Furness

Malcolm T Handley, Aylesbury

Peter Hardman, Poulton-le-Fylde

Eric Hunter, Station Square

Rose Illingworth, Cartmel

Ann James, Meadow Bank Lane

Sydney Jewsbury, Windermere

Peter A Jackson, Blackpool

Jeff Kenyon, USA

Mrs Christine Kirkman, Cart Lane

Kathleen Lister, Allithwaite

Mr & Mrs K H Leadbetter, Meadowbank Fell

Miss J L Luisa, Eden Park Road

Mrs Pat Lowrie, Lindale

John Lynch, Whalley

Harold Roe Lees, Kent's Bank

Rex Lancaster, Kent's Bank

Cllr. Mrs Pamela Monkhouse, Grange Fell Road

Marian F Mason, Kent's Bank

Susanna & David Mycock, The Esplanade

Ron & Joyce Moss, Carter Road

Robert McKeown, Leeds

Peter & Nancy Mallinson, Allithwaite Road

Anne Milligan, Rockwell Gdns

Edith Marwood-Sherwin, Skipton

J Leslie Moorhouse, Great Heads Road

Mrs Marion MacFarlane, J.P., Riggs Close

The Right Revd. Nigel McCulloch, Bishop of Wakefield

Thomas & Avril McHale, Cartmel

Malcolm & Pauline Mariam, Greenacres

David & Paulene Orrell, Kent's Bank

Gerald Owen, Greenacres

Dr David & Mrs Brenda Pearson, Eggerslack

Alan Pennington, Stockport

Miss Maureen A Porter, Carter Road

Margaret Pollard, Fence, Burnley

Emma Paul, Kent's Bank

Christine Ann Purcell, Allithwaite

Mrs Peggy Phillips, Cartmel

Mrs Lindsey Parton, Flookburgh

Andrew M Pomfret, Main Street

Mrs Marie Pearson, nee Trapp, Kendal

John Phillips, London

Stewart Platts, Arnside

Mrs Pat Rowland, Kentsford Road

L J Robinson, Allithwaite

Mr & Mrs J L Rhodes, Fulwood, Preston

Valerie Rath, Allithwaite
Kevin H Robinson, Wallasey
Miss D N Roberts, Kent's Bank
Peter Robinson, The Esplanade
M Patricia Rye, Kent's Bank
Dr Stanley Raymond, Lindale
F C Routledge, Levens
June Read, Clare House
David S Read, Clare House
Cedric Robinson, Guide's Farm
Veronica & John Rickard, Lismore, NSW
Mrs Edna Slater, Hampsfell Road
Bill & Edith Smitham, Kent's Bank
Vera & Jack Sheldon, Carter Road
S A Stevenson, Yew Tree Road
Mr & Master J N Syrett, Ashford
Mrs Robina Smith, Arnside
Joe & Marjorie Swinbank, Barnard Castle
David T Shepherd, Fell Drive
Joan Sweet, High Wycombe
John & Bernice Smithson, Wakefield
Freda A Smith, Main Street
Thomas Smith, Main Street
Ges Solway, Otley
Mrs B Shepherd, Kent's Bank
The Town Council of Grange-over-Sands
Mrs J Tomlinson, Fernhill Road
Mrs Joan Taylor, Rockland Road
Jeanne Tattersall, Lymehurst Hotel
Margaret Thomas, Allithwaite
Mrs E M Townley, Cartmel

Rosina Mary Telford, Windermere
Stuart Tyson, Saskatchewan
John M Turner, St Annes-on-Sea
Dr Michael Trenouth, Preston
Margaret & Bob Tyson, Fell Close
W Tyler, Netherleigh Drive
Mrs J E Wilson, Cartmel
Mrs M A Walmesley, Fernleigh Road
Rev. Brian Wright, Kirkhead Road
I D Wilson, Rockland Road
David Walmesley, Flookburgh
Adrian Wakefield, Methven Road
R T Walker, Haverthwaite
Derek Ward, Grange-over-Sands
Andrew Ward, Grange-over-Sands
Jonathan Ward, Grange-over-Sands
David & Emma Wheatcroft, Windermere
  Road
Nigel Wright, Cartmel
Russell Waite, Newton-in-Cartmel
Mrs Hilda Waite, Allithwaite
Keith & Jean Wright, Grange Fell Road
Mrs Kathleen Watson, Kent's Bank Road
Peter John Watson, Kent's Bank Road
Eric Charles Watson, Castle Douglas
Mrs Dilys Walker, Fleetwood
Mrs Beryl Whittaker, Chorley
David Whitehead, Wakefield
Bill & Irene Walsh, Peterborough
Colin Wong, Station Square
Mrs Ros Yates, Grantham